WESTERN WISHES

A SWEET COUNTRY ROMANCE

CAROLYNE AARSEN

CHAPTER ONE

*I*t had been many months and many miles since he'd driven this road to Refuge Ranch. A lot of memories and a lot of pain.

Tanner Fortier's foot hit the brakes as he stopped his truck at the top of the hill, a cloud of snow swirling around his vehicle. From this vantage point he looked across the basin cradling Refuge Ranch to the mountains beyond; their gray, forbidding surfaces softened by the winter snowpack, a hard white against the endless blue of the Alberta sky.

He shivered a moment, the chill of winter easing into the cab of his pickup. The side windows hadn't completely cleared of frost since Lethbridge.

Tanner stacked his gloved hands on the steering wheel, reinforcing his defenses before descending into the valley and the Bannister Ranch. He hadn't come willingly. He would have preferred to go directly home to the Circle C Ranch. Though he hadn't been away from his childhood home as long as from the Bannister ranch, he would have liked to spend some time there, catch his breath before coming here.

But time wasn't on his side, and he wanted this job out of the way.

He rolled his shoulder, tensing against the pain that knifed through it, a souvenir from a rank saddle bronc who had spun in when Tanner expected him to spin out. Tanner had lost his seat but, as if to add insult to injury, had also received a well-placed kick that had dislocated his shoulder and put him out of the money for that particular rodeo and had ruined his saddle.

Monty Bannister had been the one who made that saddle, and Tanner wanted Monty to be the one to fix it. Hence his trip here first. The sooner the saddle was fixed, the sooner Tanner could head out on the road again.

The fact that Keira Bannister, his old girlfriend and fiancée, was back living at Refuge Ranch was something he'd have to deal with.

Tanner sent up a quick prayer for strength, put his truck in gear and headed down the road. He wouldn't be long. Just a quick chat with Monty, drop off his saddle, say hello to his step-mother, who was staying at the Bannister ranch to help Ellen Bannister recuperate from a serious surgery and then head back to the Circle C Ranch a few miles down the road.

It had been his home ever since his father married Alice when he was five.

But not anymore.

Tanner had figured on staying at the Circle C for the few days it took for his saddle to be repaired and then heading back to his garage in Lethbridge, then off to his buddy's ranch near Vegas to get ready for the National Finals Rodeo. The super bowl of rodeos. The big one.

The rodeo that would, hopefully, help him let go of the burden that had been haunting him the past two years.

He cut through a grove of snow-laden pines then slowed as he entered the draw sheltering the ranch buildings. Refuge Ranch looked so much the same it gave him an ache. And yet, as he looked over the familiar gathering of barns, hay sheds, bunkhouse, and main house, he noticed a new addition. Tucked behind a grove of trees, to the left of the main house was another house that had been built while he was gone.

Was it Keira's? he wondered as he pulled into the yard.

Then, as he made that final turn, he saw her.

Her face was hidden by a misshapen cowboy hat pulled low over her head and a red knitted scarf wound around her neck. A too large, worn oilskin coat flapped around her legs, meeting laced sheepskin boots.

It could have been anyone.

Except Tanner knew that sideways tilt of her head, how she always bunched her hands inside the sleeves of her coats. How, even bundled in winter clothes, he recognized the way her purposeful stride ate up the ground.

His heart gave an unwelcome thump and his foot hit the brake too hard. His truck slid a foot or two on the packed snow, then came to a halt just as Keira Bannister looked up.

He knew the moment she saw him. Her hands fell out of her sleeves and dropped to her sides. Her narrow chin came up and her lips thinned. Even though her bangs hung well over her eyes, he caught a glitter in their blue depths that matched the chill of the sky above them. She looked angry, which puzzled him, which, in turn, made him angry.

She was the one who had broken up with him. He was the one who, if his life was a country song, had been done wrong. What right did she have to be angry?

He was the one who had tried to get them back together after their breakup when he'd returned from that string of rodeos they'd fought about. But when he'd come back to Aspen Valley, she'd disappeared. Hadn't responded to any of his calls, emails or texts. Absolute silence. And on top of that, she hadn't even bothered showing up at his stepbrother's funeral two years ago. Keira had known Roger almost as well as she'd known Tanner. But in no way did she acknowledge the loss of Tanner's stepbrother and rodeo partner. She hadn't bothered to send a note, a card, not even the courtesy of a simple text message.

What right did she have to look so angry?

Their gazes held a moment and despite the raft of negative feelings the sight of her created, woven through them all was an emotion older and deeper than that new anger and frustration. An emotion that had grown and matured as they grew up together as friends, confidants, and then sweethearts.

Tanner swallowed, as if the tightening of his throat could keep those older feelings from rising. He was surprised at how easily they returned when he saw her. He had heard, via his stepmother, Alice, that Keira had come back to Aspen Valley two years ago. A month after Roger's funeral.

He knew nothing more than that. After Roger's death, Tanner had had no reason to return to Aspen Valley so he had stayed away, working in the mechanic business that had been part of the reason he and Keira had broken up.

He took a deep breath, clapped his hat on his head and stepped out of the pickup into the chill wind that whistled down from the mountains. The sooner he got this done, the sooner he could be on his way.

He closed his truck door, tugged on his gloves, turned up the collar of his woolen coat against the cold wind that cut through the yard and walked toward Keira.

She watched him as he came, her head up, her mouth still a tight line, her cheeks a rosy glow. Blond strands of hair had slipped free from her hat and caught the wind, waving in front of her face. She batted them away, her eyes on him.

Beautiful as ever.

He caught the errant thought and pushed it back into the past.

"Hey, Keira," he said as he approached her. He stopped

4

himself from adding the ubiquitous *how are you doing* because it seemed superfluous.

"Hey, Tanner," was her tight reply, her breath creating wisps of vapor tugged by the wind as she tucked her wayward hair back under her hat. She reached down and petted her dog, Sugar, on his head, then shot another look at Tanner.

Sugar released a gentle whine, then trotted over to Tanner and sniffed at him. Then she sat down, looking up as if expecting something from him.

"Hey, Sugar," Tanner said, petting the dog, who seemed happier to see him than Keira did.

He looked back at her. They stood facing each other a moment, like combatants trying to decide who would make the first move. Guess it was up to him. "How's your mother feeling?" he asked as Sugar stretched, then returned to Keira's side.

"Today is a better day, according to your mom." She angled her chin toward the main ranch house. "You going in to see Alice? She's there right now."

"I will in a few minutes." Tanner's stepmother was a home care nurse, and right now her job was taking care of Keira's mother, Ellen Bannister, as well as babysitting Adana, John's little girl. John Argall was the ranch's hired hand. Ellen used to do the babysitting until she broke her neck in a freak fall and was now recuperating under Alice's supervision. "I'm actually here to see Monty. He around?"

Keira shoved her hands back in her sleeves as her hair came free again. "He went to Aspen Valley to get the mail and meet up with his cronies at the Grill and Chill. You can call him on his cell."

Tanner did a double take. "Monty has a cell phone? Those are words I never thought I'd hear." He couldn't imagine Monty, a hidebound Luddite and proud of it, packing a cell phone.

"Yeah. He got it when Mom had her neck fusion surgery done." Keira's hesitant tone generated a thrum of sympathy.

"I was sorry to hear about the accident," Tanner said. "Must have been scary."

"It was. We're thankful that nothing...nothing worse happened. It was a bad fall."

Keira's gaze ticked over his, and for a moment he wondered if she was going to say anything about Roger. Though two years had passed since the accident that killed his stepbrother, Keira and Tanner hadn't seen each other since his death.

But nothing.

Instead, Keira lifted her chin, staring directly at him. Her challenging attitude disturbed him, but it hurt him more. "What do you need to see my dad about?"

"I have a saddle I want him to fix," Tanner said. "Maybe I can drop it off and he can call me later?"

"Dad doesn't do much leather work anymore," was Keira's curt reply.

This was a surprise. Monty had been in the saddle-making business since he was a boy. He had learned the craft from his father and was a sought-after leather artisan. He had crafted numerous saddles given as awards in rodeos all over the Western states. The last Tanner had heard, Refuge Ranch Leatherworks was still a going concern. "I didn't think your dad would quit until someone dragged him out of here. When did that happen?"

"Since the doctor told him to slow down, and I took over."

Tanner frowned at that, trying to process this information.

"If you want your saddle looked at, I'm the one you need to talk to," Keira said. Then she spun around and ducked into the shop, Sugar right on her heels. Tanner wasn't sure whether her abrupt departure meant the conversation was over or that he should follow her into the shop.

He assumed the latter, returned to his truck and pulled the bronc saddle out of the cab. He walked to the shop and stepped inside.

After the glare of the sun on the snow outside, Tanner had to pause and let his vision adjust to the darker interior. He pulled his hat off then looked around the space of a shop that was once as familiar to him as his own home. He would often keep Keira company here when she did piecework for her father. He'd loved watching as she cut and stitched and did the intricate leather tooling on the saddles Monty was known for.

Neither Keira's older brother, Lee, or her adopted sister, Heather, were interested in the business their father had taken over from his father. Heather's focus was barrel racing at first, then modeling and Lee... Well, Lee liked his fun, running around with his buddy Mitch and, at times, Tanner's step-brother, Roger.

Now Heather was living the high-life and Lee was out of prison but not living in Aspen Valley.

Lots of sorrow for the Bannister family.

Keira was moving some pieces of cut leather off the heavy butcher-block worktable dominating the center of the building as Tanner set the saddle on it.

Across from the table, rows of shelves stacked with boxes holding grommets, snaps, buckles, and rigging D's and other hardware necessary for saddle making filled most of the wall. Beside the shelves hung stirrups made of metal or leather-covered wood, all lined up by size and shape. Next to them stood an old rolltop desk that held binders of photos of completed projects to show prospective customers.

Sugar lay on an old worn rug lying by the chair as she always did when Keira worked here.

The other corner of the shop was taken up by three industrial sewing machines. Beside them, perched on a saddle rack, was a half-finished saddle.

What had changed most was the wall opposite him. Monty used to hang pictures of finished saddles on it. Now shelves holding wallets, belts, briefcases, and purses took up that space. Obviously, a new venture for Refuge Ranch Leatherworks.

Keira brushed a few remnants of leather from the table, then adjusted a pile of cardboard patterns. Fussy work that kept her attention off him.

"Since when did you start cutting, stitching, and stamping again?" Tanner asked, slipping his hands in the pockets of his jacket.

"When I came back. About two years ago."

And a month after Roger's funeral, he had discovered. Once again he wondered why she hadn't attended the funeral. Once again the pain of her absence cut. He brushed the old feelings aside. They belonged to a past he'd closed the door on a long time ago.

"Looks like you've got a few other projects in the pipeline," he said.

Keira rested her hands on the table in front of her, looking resolutely ahead at the wall of manufactured items Tanner guessed were made right here by her. "I've been taking the business in another direction," was all she said. "Working on a purse for Freya. Brooke wants one too." She stopped, pressing her lips together, as if she had told him too much about her friends.

"Pretty ambitious. Do you still do saddles?"

"I do a few. Dad helps out, and helps me with the small work from time to time. He can't stay completely out of it." Her gaze skittered off him and onto the saddle now lying on the table between them. "That looks ragged."

Tanner ran his hand over the misshapen cantle and adjusted the worn stirrups. "Last ride was a bit of a rodeo, if you'll pardon the expression." If it were his saddle, he would have junked it. But this saddle held deep-seated memories, and he wanted it, no, needed it fixed.

Keira shot him a frown. "You still riding? I thought you were done when Alice helped you buy that mechanic shop in Lethbridge?"

"I was, but I thought I'd take one more run at the NFR this year."

Before his stepbrother died, Roger had qualified for the National Finals Rodeo in Las Vegas. After his death and after Tanner got over his grief, he promised himself he would do one last rodeo season in Roger's honor, aiming to qualify for the NFR himself. This was that season and he had done well. He felt that God had honored his request to ride in the NFR for Roger. Had some good rides and made some good money. He'd gotten some injuries on his quest, but soon he would be riding in Vegas, and he was determined to do it on Roger's saddle.

He was equally determined to win. Maybe then he could lay his guilt over Roger's death to rest.

Maybe Alice would finally forgive him.

"Wow, it certainly got a working over," she said, examining the saddle carefully.

Her throaty voice was even. Well-modulated. If anyone were listening, they would think she was talking to a stranger.

Not her former fiancé.

"The horse I drew was a bad spinner," Tanner said. "Should have known when he looked back at me with those beady brown eyes. I thought I had him from the mark out but then he set me up. When he rolled back, everything went south. Landed on the saddle and fought for a while. Worst of it all, I was riding slack. Wasn't even a performance." Tanner caught himself mid-explanation, aware that he was talking too much. It was a problem he had when he was nervous. He shut his mouth, then caught Keira's puzzled look.

"You hurt your shoulder?" she asked.

Tanner hadn't even realized he'd rolled his injured shoulder till she pointed it out. "It's nothing." It was more than nothing, but he didn't want her sympathy.

If she cared enough to give it.

Keira gave him a curt nod as she continued her inspection.

Tanner cleared his throat, wishing he felt less self-conscious in Keira's presence. He'd struggled for the past six years to forget her. To forget how she had chosen to walk away from him without a word, without a response to his request to reconcile their broken engagement. An engagement she had called off. It had been a long, hard-won victory over his emotions and his past, and even despite losing Roger, he felt as if he had come to a better place in his life. A place where he could look ahead instead of always thinking about the "could-have-beens."

Coming back here was a test for him. Keira's continued hold on his heart had been preventing him from building new relationships.

He had hoped that by seeing Keira again he might finally be able to put her place in his life in perspective. Maybe even rid himself of her ever-present shadow.

Trouble was, now that he saw her again, he wasn't sure if that was even possible.

KEIRA WISHED she could keep her hands from trembling as she handled the saddle under Tanner's watchful gaze. What was wrong with her? She was prepared for Tanner's arrival. Alice, Tanner's stepmother, had mentioned it a couple of days ago. Had even given a date.

Yet, seeing him now, his brown eyes edged with sooty lashes and framed by the slash of dark brows, the hard planes of his face emphasized by the stubble shadowing his jaw and cheeks, brought back painful memories Keira thought she had put aside.

He looked the same and yet different. Harder. Leaner. He wore his sandy brown hair longer, brushing the collar of his shirt, giving him a reckless look at odds with the Tanner she had once known.

And loved.

She sucked in a rapid breath as she turned over the saddle, the wooden stirrups thumping dully on the table. Tanner seemed to fill the cramped shop, and Keira sensed his every movement.

Keep your focus on your work, she reminded herself, pulling her attention back to the broken saddle she was examining.

"So? What's the verdict, Latigo Kid?" Tanner asked.

His casual use of the old nickname he always used for her caught her off guard. And when her startled gaze caught his surprised one, she guessed the name had fallen out unintentionally.

She dragged her attention back to the saddle. "I don't know if it's worth fixing this," she said quietly, examining the bottom, then the stirrup leathers. "Back billet is broken. The swell cover is ripped and it looks pretty rough. You've worked it over pretty good with that wire brush."

"Resin stays on better that way."

Keira acknowledged his comment with a quick nod. Saddle bronc riders often sprinkled resin on their saddles to help them stay seated. The wire brush roughed up the leather, so the resin stuck better.

"The stirrup leathers should be replaced," she said, continuing her litany of repairs. "You'll need new latigos, and the D rings need to be reattached if not replaced. It'll be a lot of work."

Tanner sighed as he tugged his gloves off and shoved them in the pocket of his worn plaid jacket. "But can you fix it?"

"I'd need to take it apart to see. It might need a whole new tree. If that's the case, two weeks?" She was pleased at how even her voice sounded. At how businesslike she could be. As if he was simply another customer.

"That's cutting it close," Tanner said, scratching his cheek with his index finger. "I know you've got other projects going on, but is it possible to get it done quicker?"

Keira would have preferred not to work on it at all. It would mean that, instead of him dropping in to say hello to his mother and then leaving, Tanner would be around more often so she could fit the saddle and make the necessary adjustments.

It had taken her years to relegate Tanner to the shadowy recesses of her mind. She didn't know if she could maintain any semblance of the hard-won peace she now experienced if she had to see him more often. Tanner was too ingrained in her past and too connected to memories she had spent hours in prayer trying to bury.

"I'm gonna need it for the National Finals in Vegas," Tanner continued. "I was hoping to practice on it before that."

"Your mother said you had qualified. That's quite a feat." Keira knew this from comments Alice dropped here and there, but overall, Alice kept most news of Tanner to herself, and Keira didn't press for more. She knew she had no right to know what was going on in Tanner's life. Not after she'd left him the way she had.

She also knew Alice had been curious. But Keira wasn't about to let her know everything.

"I placed third overall in the regular season," Tanner said. "Missed a few rodeos 'cause of injuries, so I'm hoping to do better in Vegas."

Tanner and his stepbrother, Roger, had ridden the rodeo together since they first qualified as novices. They had both ridden saddle broncs and competed in the same rodeos, often working their way up the ranks together.

In fact, it was Tanner's involvement in rodeo that had been one of the points of contention between them when she and Tanner were dating. She hated watching him risk his life each time he mounted a saddle bronc.

She also hated the fact that after his father died, instead of working on the Circle C Ranch with Roger and his step-mother, he had taken a job working as a mechanic's appren-tice. Between his work and rodeoing, they'd hardly seen each other. She had always thought he would partner up with Roger to work on his father's ranch. He'd been working on it since his father married Alice and moved in when Tanner was five.

But after Cyrus Fortier died, Tanner went to work full-time as a mechanic.

He couldn't get work in Aspen Valley or Calgary, and ended up working for a mechanic in Lethbridge, a four-hour drive from the ranch. They had fought bitterly about that.

She hated the long-distance. Hated that he didn't want to live in Aspen Valley. Couldn't figure out why he'd sooner work as a mechanic than on the ranch, and he wouldn't explain himself to her.

"I heard you're still doing mechanic work, as well?"

"Still pulling wrenches. But I own the shop now."

"Where is it?"

"The same one I started working at before—" He cut himself off there but didn't need to finish. Keira knew exactly what he meant.

Before that summer when she left Tanner's ring behind. When she left Tanner and Aspen Valley, without telling him why. Before that summer when everything changed.

A heavy silence dropped between them as solid as a wall. Keira turned away, pushing the memories down again. Burying them deep where they couldn't taunt her.

But Tanner's very presence teased them to the surface.

Dear Lord, help me through this situation. I don't have enough strength on my own.

She looked up at him to tell him she couldn't work on the saddle, but as she did, she felt a jolt of awareness. In his eyes she saw puzzlement and hurt. She tried to tear her gaze away, but it was as if the old bond that had once connected them still bound them to each other.

Her resolve weakened and against her better judgment she took another look at the saddle, weighing, judging. "I don't know…" Her voice trailed off. She wasn't sure she wanted to have anything more to do with Tanner than she could possibly avoid. Fixing his saddle would put them in each other's paths far too often.

"I'd appreciate it if you could fix it. It means a lot to me." His conciliatory tone, so at odds with the faint mockery that had laced his words previously, caught her off guard.

She sighed, wondering again if she was letting sentiment dictate her actions. She turned the saddle over again, looking at it more closely. Then she frowned.

"This saddle has some initials stamped on it," she said quietly, turning the leather of the skirt over to show him. "I can't make it out."

"R.F. Roger Fortier. It was my stepbrother's saddle."

Roger's saddle. Keira's heart, already overworked, kicked up another notch. "Why are you using it?" She jerked her hands away.

"In honor of him. We were getting to the end of the season when he died. He had qualified for the NFR. I promised myself to finish what he started. It took me two years, but here I am."

Keira looked the saddle over then shook her head. "I'm sorry, Tanner. I can't fix it for you."

"What? Why not?" Tanner shot her a frustrated scowl. "I thought you said it would take two weeks."

"I don't think I can find two weeks to work on it. I'll get you the card of someone who might be able to help you," she said, turning her back to him as she rummaged through the old wooden desk, her hands trembling again as she pulled a business card out of one of the drawers.

Sugar, startled out of her sleep, stood and looked up at her, the dog's head tilted to one side as if wondering what she was doing.

Keira took a deep breath, sent up another prayer then handed the card to Tanner.

He took it, then frowned. "Landolt?"

"He does good work."

"Not as good as Monty. And you."

Keira's hand lowered as she looked from the card Tanner held to the saddle laying on the table. It was as if that inanimate object encapsulated so much of what lay between her and Tanner. And what could never be changed.

"There's another guy in southern B.C., close to Sweet Creek, who Dad refers people to," she said, turning back to her desk. "I'll see if I have his information."

Just then the door of the shop opened, bringing in the chill of the outdoors and a flash of sunlight. Sugar jumped up and ran to the door.

"Well, well. If it isn't Tanner Fortier." Her father's voice boomed into the silence as he shut the door behind him, closing off the cold and the light.

Keira turned in time to see Tanner enveloped in a bear hug by her tall, lean father. Monty was easily six feet tall, but Tanner topped him by a couple of inches. Monty pulled back, shaking his head as he looked Tanner over. "You look like some cast-away cowboy," he teased, clapping a hand on Tanner's worn jacket.

"I feel like one," Tanner retorted as a truly genuine smile softened his harsh features, put a sparkle in his dark eyes and disturbed Keira's equilibrium. "Been a busy season."

"You did well, I understand. Enough to qualify for the NFR. Good stuff. Proud of you, son." Monty beamed his approval. He had always liked Tanner. Solid, dependable. Hardworking.

An overall great guy. Someone Monty easily called son as he had while he and Keira were dating. When they got engaged,

15

her parents were thrilled. Part of that happiness was because Monty and Ellen needed some good news in their lives. Their oldest son, Lee, had just been sent to prison, and Keira's older sister, Heather, had just moved to New York against their wishes. The engagement of a Bannister to a Fortier had been the one bright spot in that horrible year.

Keira's heart stuttered again.

"And what do we have here?" Monty was saying as he picked up the saddle. "Not this saddle's first rodeo."

"I brought it here hoping you could fix it."

Monty turned the saddle over and smiled. "I made this one," he said. "For your brother, Roger."

"I was just telling Tanner that we don't have time to work on it," Keira said, praying again as she caught Tanner's confused gaze in her peripheral vision.

"Of course we have time," he said, his frown showing her he didn't get her unspoken message. "For Tanner, we make time."

"We've got an exhibition to get stuff ready for and that order from that store in Seattle," Keira replied, wishing she could keep the pleading tone out of her voice. She had no concrete reason not to do the job, nor was she about to get into specifics.

"Get Isabelle Cosgrove to come in and help you," Monty said. "I'm sure she wouldn't mind some extra hours. Or I can pitch in."

"The doctor said you had to slow down. I don't want you working too much."

Monty waved off her concerns then turned to Tanner. "Just leave it here, son. We'll get it fixed up for you one way or the other."

Keira maintained a veneer of tense restraint, but she felt it slipping. She wasn't going to look at Tanner, but as if her eyes had their own will, they slid in his direction.

It wasn't hard to see the hurt and puzzlement on his face,

and for a moment she prayed for a return to the muted anger he had shown when he'd first come in.

That would be easier to deal with.

God had been her refuge and strength the past few years. Her strong fortress. And from the way events were moving now, she would need His strength more than ever in the next few weeks.

CHAPTER TWO

"You better come up to the house," Monty said as Keira moved the saddle over to the workbench.

Tanner shot another look at Keira, still baffled at her hesitation, but then turned his attention back to Monty. "Yes. I'd like to see how Ellen's doing," he said.

"And your mother," Monty added. "She's been looking forward to your visit."

Tanner doubted that. He and his stepmother had never been close and less so since Roger's death. She had never come out and said it, but he knew she blamed him for the accident. And why not? Tanner blamed himself, as well. If he had been more insistent, he would have been driving his stepbrother back to the hotel. And both he and Roger would have made it safely to Cheyenne.

"Are you coming, Keira?" Monty asked as he dropped his worn cowboy hat on his head.

"Maybe later. I've got to cut out some wallets before I quit for the day."

"Can't that wait?" Monty asked.

"No. Not if we have to work on Tanner's saddle, too." Keira's unexpectedly sharp tone grated on Tanner. But he shook off his frustration.

He'd gotten his first visit with Keira out of the way. Though he'd hoped his heart wouldn't race at the sight of her, at least that was done. Maybe next time he saw her, he would feel more even-keeled.

Help me, Lord, he prayed as he clapped his hat on his head. *Help me get through this emotional tangle.*

He turned up the collar of his jacket and followed Monty out the door and over the snow-covered yard to the house, shivering as he stepped from the warmth of the shop into the chill of the outside air. *Help me get through the next couple of days. Help me stay focused on what I set out to do.*

He felt guilty praying to God right now. Living the life of a rodeo cowboy wasn't always conducive to a robust spiritual life. Too many late nights. Too many weekends taken up with riding and work and getting over injuries. Then back to work, only to repeat the same weekend cycle.

But he knew God was real, and right now he needed all the help he could get.

The snow squeaked under their feet, showing him how cold it was outside. Tanner looked out over the hills blanketed with snow undulating to mountains sharply etched against a sky so blue it hurt his eyes. Gray clouds were piling up on the horizon, hinting at potential winter storms.

But for now, the sun shone on Refuge Ranch, sparkling off the snow-covered hills.

"The house won't be as noisy as usual," Monty explained as they walked toward it. "Ellen usually takes care of John's little girl, but he's got her today. He's doing some bookwork in his house."

"I heard that Samantha died two days after Adana was born. That's a sad story."

"It is. But Adana's a little treasure and we're all crazy about her. Taking care of her is a small price to pay to have John able to keep working here. His father was the best hand a rancher could ask for, and John has the same cattle smarts his father did."

"John was always a good, solid guy," Tanner said. "I always thought he and Heather were a better match than her and Mitch."

"Didn't we all," Monty said, shooting Tanner a look, as if he was thinking the same thing about him and Keira.

Tanner kept his comments to himself. No sense in digging up the past.

They walked up the steps, and Tanner pulled open the door to the porch.

"Got company," Monty boomed as the porch door fell shut behind them.

Warmth from the adjoining kitchen slowly penetrated the many layers of clothing Tanner had on. He stripped off his coat and hung it and his hat on an empty hanger in the porch. Then he toed off his boots, set them aside and followed Monty into the familiar coziness of the ranch house.

"We fixed up the kitchen since you been here," Monty said as he led Tanner through the room as familiar to him as the kitchen on his parents' ranch. "Ellen had a notion she wanted some fancy new stove and fridge and granite countertops. Place looks like a dairy barn with all these shiny appliances far as I'm concerned," he said, waving a dismissive hand at the stainless-steel stove, refrigerator, and dishwasher. "At least she kept the table in the nook."

A large bay window with French doors opening to a snow-covered deck was home to a small wooden table with mismatched chairs that, Tanner knew, were part of Monty's father and grandfather's ranch house that this house had replaced.

"Still looks cozy," Tanner said, stopping by the table. He

remembered drinking many a cup of hot chocolate in the winter or root beer in the summer at this table when he and Keira were dating. Refuge Ranch had truly lived up to its name when his own home had been a place of discord and conflict. Tanner's father, Cyrus, had married Alice less than a year after his wife's death, when Tanner was only five. Roger was born within the first year of that marriage. While Roger and Tanner always got along, Tanner remembered many fights between Cyrus and Alice, though he never knew the cause.

Yet despite their antagonism, somehow Alice had inherited the entire ranch when Cyrus died. Tanner had suspected that his father had neglected to change his will as he had always promised Tanner he would. To be fair, Tanner wasn't his father's natural son. Tanner's mother had come into the marriage with him when he was just a newborn.

But Cyrus had always told him he would make sure he was taken care of.

Tanner had foolishly assumed that would mean he would be part owner of the ranch he had worked on his whole life.

He hadn't figured it would mean that when push came to shove biology took precedence over promises.

But shortly after the funeral, Roger had broken it to him that their father had willed the ranch to him. Roger offered Tanner the opportunity to work it as well.

Tanner had been devastated but, in the end, not so surprised. When Roger was born, there had been a definite shift in his father's attitude toward him. And with every passing year, Roger became the obvious favorite.

Tanner had kept the shame and pain of it to himself after his father's death, unable to tell Keira. He didn't know how to break the news to her.

All throughout their courtship she talked about moving to the Fortier ranch and how they would fix it up. Tanner knew how much she loved the wide-open spaces of the ranch and the valley. He knew how hard it would be for her to move into town.

Too proud to tell her exactly why he wasn't going to be living on the ranch after his father died, he started work as a mechanic, trying to scrape enough money together to find a small place outside town and still find a way for him to make a living. Weekends were spent rodeoing. Things had slowly been coming together and he'd weathered their fights, hoping to present his plan to her once he had a place to buy. Only then did he mean to tell her about his father's will and the repercussions for them.

He'd obviously waited too long. After a long spell of work and rodeoing, he had finally worked up enough courage to tell her about Cyrus's will. He was on the road, rodeoing in Wyoming when he tried to call her. It went to voicemail, and he said he had something he needed to talk to her about.

But she didn't reply.

Then he texted her. Again, nothing.

He came back to Aspen Valley to talk to her in person, but she was gone. The only thing he got was a note she had left with her parents.

And his ring.

He hadn't heard from her since. Hadn't seen her since. He'd tried texting her best friends. Freya only told him she was worried about Keira, but nothing more. Brooke wasn't much help either. In fact, she raked him over, thinking it was his fault her friend had left town.

If it wasn't for the fact that he had Roger's saddle to fix, their paths would probably have never crossed again.

He had no reason to come back to Aspen Valley.

"Hey, ladies, look who I brought," Monty announced as they stepped into the large, exposed-beamed living room. A fire crackled in the woodstove, generating a welcome heat.

His stepmother sat on a leather easy chair, facing him, her

blond hair cut in a serviceable page boy, dark-framed glasses emphasizing her green eyes. She wore a white shirt, black chinos and sensible white shoes, all of which combined to make her look precisely like the nurse she was.

Ellen sat with her back to him, her long brown hair, tinged with gray, pulled back in a ponytail hanging over the large brace that held her neck and upper chest immobilized. She sat upright in a chair and as she slowly got to her feet, Tanner winced at the sight of the brace.

"I know, I know, I look like an alien," Ellen said, her voice sounding restricted and strained. "I hope I don't scare you too much. I'd still like a hug."

"Be careful," Monty whispered, detaining Tanner a moment. "She's still hurting."

Tanner nodded and slowly approached Ellen and, bending over, brushed a gentle kiss on her cheek. "Sorry, Ellen, that's all you get from me for now."

She smiled up at him and reached up to touch his face, then blanched in pain. "I keep thinking I can do what I used to," she said with a tone of regret. "But it's great to see you again. Though you look tired."

"Been a long drive." He smiled at her then glanced over at his stepmother. "Hello, Alice," he said.

Alice set her cup aside, brushed her hands over her pants and slowly rose to greet him, as well. That Ellen, despite her disability, was quicker to greet him than his stepmother rankled.

Alice walked over and managed a perfunctory hug then pulled back, folding her arms over her chest. "Hello, Tanner. Good to see you. How have you been?"

"Good." He struggled to think of what else to say. Since that horrible conversation when she'd accused him of causing her beloved son, Roger's death, every exchange with her was stilted and strained.

The problem was her accusations—spoken and unspoken—only underlined what he had always thought himself.

If he hadn't let Roger stay behind to spend time with that girl, if Tanner had followed his better judgment and insisted on bringing him back to the hotel, Roger would still be alive.

Monty walked over to his wife and kissed her lightly on the cheek. "How are you feeling, my dear?" Concern laced his voice and Ellen gave him a faint smile.

"Exactly the same as I did when you left two hours ago to go coffee drinking," she said, a note of humor in her voice. "Would you like some coffee, Tanner?"

"Sorry, but I'd like to get back to the ranch and catch up on some phone calls and paperwork." He caught a frown from Alice. "If that's okay?" he added.

His stepmother shook her head with an expression of regret. "I'm sorry, but you won't be able to. I thought while I was staying here and taking care of Ellen, I would get some renovations done on the house," she said. "So, it isn't livable right now. In fact, I've been staying here at the ranch the past couple of nights."

"You're saying I should stay somewhere else?"

"Might be a good idea."

To his surprise her voice held an apologetic tone that he was too tired to interpret.

"You can stay here." Monty slapped Tanner on the back. "Give you a chance to spend time with your mother, catch up with us. Keep tabs on your saddle's repair."

His stepmother didn't seem pleased with the idea, and he guessed that Keira would feel much the same.

"I don't think so," Tanner said. "I'll try to find a place in town instead."

"Don't know if you'll be able to." Monty shook his head. "There's some hockey tournament going on this next week in

Aspen Valley. Fairly sure the few hotels we got are full. So, I guess you're stuck here until something opens up."

Tanner stifled a sigh, feeling as if he was slowly getting pushed into a tight corner. Never a good place to be. "I'm not sure—"

"Not sure about what? We got plenty of room. John is staying in the house his parents used to live in, and our last hired hand quit on us so the bunkhouse is empty. You can stay there. It's all ready to go. Trust me, it's no problem."

Tanner was about to object again but felt that doing so would make him look ungrateful and un-neighborly. He eased out a smile. "Sure. I guess I can stay. I'm only here for a couple of days."

"It will take longer than that to fix Roger's saddle," Monty said. "Besides, you can help. You know a few things about saddle repair. You and Keira used to hang out at the shop all the time."

"Roger's saddle?" Alice glanced from Tanner to Monty, looking confused. "Why do you need to get it fixed?"

"I've been using it all season and it needs some work," Tanner said, looking over at his stepmother. "It got a real working over the last time I competed."

"You've been using it this year?" Alice looked surprised.

"All year," Tanner replied. "It's been a busy run."

"When are you ever going to quit the rodeo?" Ellen asked, a note of disappointment lacing her voice. "Surely your mechanic work keeps you busy enough?"

"It does. But I've got some good workers who are running the business for me. Just hired a foreman last year so I could do this one last circuit."

"Will this really be the last?" Monty gave him a wry smile. "I know you cowboys. You don't quit until you're dragged from the arena on a backboard. Surely you need to decide when the time comes..." He let the sentence fade away, but Tanner finished it for him.

"To hang up my rigging and my spurs," Tanner said. "Yeah. I know. Hopefully this year will be that year."

"Why are you using Roger's saddle?" Alice pressed. "Don't you have your own?"

Tanner was silent a moment, trying to find the right way to answer her.

"I do. But I wanted to finish what Roger started before... before he died." It had been two years since Roger's death, and those words could still cut like a knife. "I thought I would use his saddle and dedicate the season to him. I want to take the saddle all the way to the NFR. But it got busted up at the last rodeo. Monty said he would fix it for me so I could finish with it at Las Vegas."

He wished she hadn't pushed him. He had hoped to surprise her after the season was over and give her Roger's saddle as a memento. Tell her face-to-face why he did what he did. Hope that, by some miracle, she would grant him some measure of absolution.

Their eyes held and for a moment, her smile softened, and he recognized it for what it was. A small movement toward forgiveness. Then she gave a curt nod and her mouth shifted into the polite smile he knew only too well.

"I think that's admirable," she said, her tone impersonal. "I guess we'll have to see how you do in the end."

The end.

Tanner briefly wondered if there would be an end to his quest. To his desire for some type of reconciliation with her.

But now, as ever, her manner was aloof, reserved, and cool.

Time to go.

"So, the bunkhouse?" Tanner asked Monty.

"It's all fixed up. Do you want me to bring you there? It's not locked."

"I'll be fine."

"I'll come over with clean sheets for the bed," Alice said, getting up from her chair.

"Just tell me where they are. I can make a bed." She was the one who had taught him, after all.

"Of course. I'll get them for you."

She left and Tanner caught Ellen watching him, the neck and chest brace supporting her head giving her a vulnerable look. "We've missed you, Tanner. I'm glad you're staying here." Her voice, sounding so strained created an extra poignancy.

"I'm glad I'm back, too," he said quietly, though staying on the ranch with Keira so close by was not how he had envisioned his temporary stay.

His stepmother came back with a stack of sheets and some towels. "I gave you extra. Just in case."

Tanner gave her a tight nod, then took a step back. "I better get myself set up."

"And we'll see you for supper tonight?"

Resistance rose again, but the expectant looks on Monty's and Ellen's faces quashed it. Surely, he could manage this for these dear people, who had been such a part of his life so long?

"Sure. What time?"

"Come at six."

He gave them another smile, glanced over at his stepmother, who stood with her arms crossed, her stolid expression making him wonder if he had imagined that momentary bond.

A few moments later he was walking toward his truck, his breath creating clouds of fog in the chill winter air. He stopped at the truck, dug his keys out of his pocket one-handed and caught a movement from the saddle shop.

Keira stood in the doorway and his heart pounded double-time in his chest. As he looked at her, his thoughts drifted back to times he would help her in the shop, then go out for a ride in the hills. He watched her a moment, but he noticed her eyes weren't on him. They were on the mountains just beyond the edges of Refuge Ranch.

Her arms were wrapped around her midsection. Then, to his surprise, he saw her hand swipe at her cheeks.

As if she were crying.

"Excellent meal, Alice," Tanner said as he set his knife and fork on his plate and wiped his mouth with a napkin. "I haven't had a good Angus steak for ages."

"I'm glad you could be here to share it with us," Monty replied, taking another bite.

"Keira made supper," Ellen corrected, taking a careful sip of the smoothie Alice had concocted for her.

"That's great," Tanner said, glancing over at Keira. "I didn't think you enjoyed cooking."

Keira managed a half smile at his attempt to engage her in conversation, then looked back down at the steamed vegetables she'd spent the past ten minutes pushing around her plate. She knew what Tanner was thinking. Ever since she was a young girl, she would try to find a way to get out of any kind of kitchen duty. Ellen and Keira's sister, Heather, were the ones who cooked, baked, made jam, and gardened.

Keira had always been more interested in tagging along behind her father, working with him in the shop and helping him and her brother, Lee, work the cows.

Which worked out for the best. While Heather was a natural on a horse, she didn't like working with the cows.

"I've learned a few other skills lately," she said, stabbing a piece of cauliflower with her fork.

"I can see that," Tanner said.

She wanted to look at him but chose to keep her attention on the plate in front of her.

Keira, her parents, Alice and Tanner were gathered around the large table that filled the dining area tucked away in one corner of the large open main floor. The lights around them were turned low, a fire crackled and popped in the stone fireplace. Curtains were drawn across the windows, creating a peaceful and cozy ambiance.

But for Keira, the meal had been an ordeal. Tanner had ended up sitting across from her, and every time she looked up, she caught him watching her, then giving her a faintly mocking smile.

Tanner had always been someone who used sarcasm to deflect anyone getting close and could put on a cynical facade with people he didn't care for.

But he'd never been that way with her. Which was why his half smile and slightly hooded eyes created not only a deep discomfort but also a pain that she felt she had no right to experience.

"It's been a long time since I enjoyed a meal here," Tanner said, turning his attention back to Monty and Ellen. "Actually, it's been a long time since I had a home-cooked meal, period."

"I know how you feel," Ellen said, setting her smoothie down. "I'll be so happy to be off this liquid diet and sink my teeth into a juicy steak or pork chop soon."

Monty patted her lightly on the arm. "Patience is a virtue," he said with a smile.

"Spoken by the man who just finished an eight-ounce sirloin," Ellen returned with a fake glower. "But I should be thankful for small mercies. Only ten more weeks, four days, and twenty hours till this thing comes off."

"Not that you're counting," Tanner said with a grin.

"Can you tell she's a bit testy?" Monty asked. He glanced over at Keira. "Honey, are you feeling okay? You've hardly eaten anything."

"I'm not hundred percent," was her vague reply. Which was

the truth. Ever since Tanner had come into the shop, she felt as if her emotions had been tossed over like a bucket of nails she didn't know how to gather up again.

She took a bite of her now cold cauliflower, choked it down and decided to give up on eating altogether.

"Is everyone done?" she asked, glancing around the table as she reached for the bowl of potatoes.

"What's the rush?" Monty asked, stopping her by placing his hand on her arm. "We can sit awhile."

"No rush. Just want to get this cleared off," Keira said. "I want to get back to the shop to do some more work on Freya's purse."

Her father held her gaze, a faint frown wrinkling his forehead as if trying to see into her mind.

Tanner wasn't the only one who didn't know all the reasons she had left Aspen Valley all those years ago. Though she had kept in touch with her parents, she had never answered all their questions about her and Tanner's broken engagement. Her mother and father had dropped some gentle hints, but for the most part they had never probed too deeply.

"If you want to go out to the shop, I can take care of the dishes," Monty said. He got up but suddenly his cell phone beeped. He glanced at it, then emitted a huge sigh.

"Everything okay?" Ellen asked.

Monty shook his head. "Not really. Giesbrook just called John. He wants those heifers delivered tomorrow."

"You have to go to Sweet Creek on Sunday?" Keira asked, suddenly concerned.

"Not until later in the day. I'd like to get some work done on the saddle, but I won't be able to get it done." He gave her an apologetic look. "Do you mind finishing it up for me?"

Keira glared at her father. She did mind and he knew it. If she didn't know better, she would have guessed he'd engineered this change in plans. But what else could she say with

Tanner right there? Instead, she nodded and started stacking the plates.

"I told you I'd do that, honey," Monty said.

"No, you can't," Ellen protested. "You promised me and Alice a game of Scrabble after dinner." Ellen glanced over at Tanner. "Tanner, do you mind helping Keira?"

"Never been too proud to do dishes," Tanner said, getting to his feet, giving Keira a careful smile. But from the tightness of Tanner's lips, she guessed he was as unwilling to be around her as she was to be around him.

Though she could hardly blame him. She was the one who left without a word after all. While Tanner? Well, he'd done nothing wrong.

Except change the plans they had made.

She pushed the unfair thought aside. Though he never told her the reason for him not working the Circle C with Roger after his father died, she had thought they could find a way to make their own way.

Then everything fell apart.

They cleared the dishes as Ellen, Monty, and Alice retreated to a corner of the living room that held the game table. Monty held Ellen's arm, guiding her awkward steps, but they made it to the table without mishap.

"Your mom seems frustrated," Tanner said as they brought the dishes to the kitchen. "Not like her usual bubbly self."

"She's fragile and can't do much for herself, but she hasn't complained yet." Keira stacked the plates by the sink and started cleaning them.

"I'm sure having Alice around helps a lot."

"She's helpful. Of course, part of the reason she's staying here is because of her house getting fixed up."

"I thought Alice was here to help your mother," Tanner responded.

"She is, but she doesn't need to be here twenty-four seven."

She didn't mind Alice but having her around day and night was tiring. Now and again, she would catch Alice looking at her as if she wasn't sure what to make of Keira.

Truth to tell, it was kind of creepy.

She busied herself with scraping the leftover food off the plates. Tanner left to get more dishes and she took a deep breath, chiding herself for being such a wimp around him. Goodness, it had been years since they had seen each other. Surely, she could get over this.

Tanner returned to the kitchen, and over the clink of cutlery and the swish of water over the plates, the only other sound was the muted laughter from Monty, Ellen, and Alice playing Scrabble in the other room.

Keira reached for a plate just as Tanner did, and when their hands brushed, Keira jumped. She dropped the plate the same time he did, and it clattered to the floor, shattering on the slate tile.

"Sorry."

"My fault."

They both spoke at once, both knelt at once and both tried to pick up the broken pieces at the same time.

Flustered, Keira grabbed blindly at a shard, which immediately cut into her hand. She yanked it back as blood dripped onto the floor.

"Here, let me help you with that," Tanner said, catching her hand to hold it still.

She tried to pull back, which only made the blood flow more freely. "I can take care of this." She didn't want him touching her. Didn't want him so close to her.

"Hold still," Tanner said, frowning as they both stood up. "Where's your first-aid kit?"

"It's nothing. Just a small cut." She tried once again to pull her hand free, but she had forgotten how strong and stubborn he could be.

Tanner's mouth thinned into a grim line. "Just tell me where the bandages are," he growled.

"Is everything okay in there?" Keira heard her father call out.

"Just fine," Tanner yelled back. Then he turned to Keira, grabbed a towel and wrapped it tightly around her hand. He made her sit down at the small table in the breakfast nook. "Now. Bandages?"

"There's a first-aid kit in the bottom drawer of the island. Far left side."

"Good girl." He strode to the island, retrieved the kit, then brought it back to the table. He opened it, then found what he needed.

"Give me your hand," he said, his voice now quiet as he ripped open a bandage.

Keira tamped down her reaction and held her hand out to him. He knelt in front of her, carefully removed the towel, dabbed at the cut as he examined it. "You won't need stitches," he said as he quickly wrapped a bandage around the wound. "But you'll need at least two bandages."

Keira tried to distract herself from his large hands gently maneuvering the second bandage onto her cut. She felt the calluses on his palms, caught the familiar scent of the aftershave he used, the smell of the shampoo he used. The overhead light shone on his hair, bringing out a faint sheen of gold in the brown, and Keira found she had to make a fist of her free hand to stop herself from reaching up and smoothing it away from his face.

The way she always used to.

Just then he looked up and their eyes met. Held.

His expression softened. She couldn't look away and for a moment it was as if all the years between them, all the events that kept them apart, had been erased.

"Is everything okay?"

33

Alice stood in the doorway of the kitchen; her arms folded over her chest.

And her presence brought stark reality back into the moment.

"I...I cut myself," Keira murmured, pulling her hand out of Tanner's.

"Oh, my. Here, let me help you," Alice said, skirting the broken dish to get to Keira.

"It's fine now," Keira said, tucking her hand against her side as she got up. "Just a cut. Tanner bandaged it up." She was about to walk back to finish the dishes when Alice stopped her.

"Why don't you take my place at the Scrabble game?" Alice said. "Tanner and I can finish up."

"Sure. That's a good idea," she said, thankful for the reprieve.

But as she walked past Tanner, she caught his cynical smile, firmly back in place.

She paused just outside the kitchen, where neither Alice and Tanner nor her parents could see her. She took a moment, leaning against the wall, trying to get her bearings.

A little help here, Lord, she prayed, willing her tangled emotions to find the peace and equilibrium she had managed to attain before Tanner had dropped back into her life.

All she had to do was get through the next few days, she reminded herself as she pinned a smile on her face and walked out to where her parents sat by the table. *Dad will get the saddle fixed and Tanner—and all the memories and pain he evoked—would be out of my life. Soon.*

CHAPTER THREE

*T*he last time he'd been in this church building was for Roger's funeral.

Tanner stood in the back of the foyer of the Aspen Valley Church, looking over the gathered people, painful memories leaning into him. He pushed away his sorrow as he thought of his father and his stepbrother, both now buried in the graveyard beside the church. For a moment he wished he hadn't come, but lately he had felt the old hunger for his faith gnawing at him.

He'd arranged to meet George Bamford, owner of the Grill and Chill, about a place he could stay while he waited for his saddle to get fixed. There was no way he was staying at Refuge Ranch another night.

So, he had two reasons to come to church this morning.

"Welcome to our services."

Tanner recognized Rolph Nielson, a man about his age, smiling, wearing a black tie and blue shirt. Though he was closer to Burke Prins' age, Tanner remembered him from school.

"Hey, Tanner," Rolph said, sounding genuinely pleased. "So great to see you back. How long you around for?"

"Couple of weeks," Tanner said, taking the bulletin.

"Well, that's nice. Welcome back. Let me find you a place to sit," Rolph said, spinning around and starting down the center aisle, giving Tanner no choice but to follow him.

He stopped at the end of a pew and gave Tanner a bulletin. Tanner gave him a quick smile, sat down, looked over and froze.

Keira had just walked in, and was moving into the same pew, sitting down beside Brooke, her old friend.

He couldn't sit here.

He was about to stand and move on to another empty spot in the opposite pew when Keira looked over at him. It would look too strange if he moved now, so he sat back into the pew, accepting his fate. He chanced another glance over at Keira, then frowned.

Her long-sleeved black T-shirt and pants and stark ponytail were a far cry from the bright colors, swirly skirts, dresses, and done-up hair that she used to favor. Many a Sunday morning he would come to Refuge Ranch to pick up Keira for church. He'd always had to wait as Keira and her sister, Heather, chose their makeup, clothing, and jewelry.

Today she looked as if she didn't want to draw attention to herself. As if she were trying to hide.

He shot her another glance, surprised to find her glance over at him. Then a flush colored her cheeks and she looked quickly away, turning back to Brooke. But her friend was leaning past her, looking at Tanner, the faint frown on her face telegraphing her disapproval of his presence there.

As if he had done something wrong.

For a moment he regretted coming. But he pulled in a breath, ignoring both of them and looking at the front of the church, centering himself. He was here to worship. He shouldn't care what Keira or her friend Brooke thought.

The worship team was assembling at the front, another surprise for Tanner. For as long as he could remember, Anita

Descant had played the old organ, coaxing maximum volume for her favorite hymns, making it barely wheeze for the songs she didn't care for. In fact, she had played for Roger's funeral, a long, steady requiem of mournful songs that had served only to make Tanner even more depressed.

But this group started a lively song that got Tanner's toe's tapping though he didn't recognize the song they were playing.

Halfway through the first song he felt a nudge on his shoulder.

"You're in my spot, young man."

He looked up, puzzled, then repressed a grin.

Nate Montane glared down at him, frowning.

He had forgotten that Mr. Montane had always sat here. His daughter, Courtney, had always taken up the space between him and Keira. But that was many years ago.

"So. You're back," Nate said, his frown easing as he recognized Tanner. "You don't usually sit here."

Tanner shook his head as he moved over to give Nate room yet still preserve some space between him and Keira. "No. Me and my family always sat in the back."

Nate dropped into the pew beside him and let out a mournful sigh, then looked past him at the space between him and Keira. "Your lucky today. Courtney, Fenna and Cole usually sit with me but they're delivering a horse."

"Courtney's here? I thought she lived in the Netherlands."

"She's back to stay. Her and her little girl. And her and Cole Waldren are married now."

Now that he mentioned it, Tanner remembered snippets of Aspen Valley gossip about Courtney and other members of the community that his mother fed him whenever he called home.

"Wow. Things are certainly changing."

"Sometimes for the good." Nate eased out a rare smile. "What you been doing since you left Aspen Valley?" Nate asked him.

"Been busy with work," Tanner said with a polite smile. He knew his sudden appearance after a two-year absence would engender commentary, welcome or not.

"You sound like Courtney," Nate replied, tugging a folded-up bulletin out of the pocket of his shirt. "She's always busy too. Got lots on the go with training her horses. But it's a good busy."

Tanner was surprised to hear the cheerful tone in Nate's voice. From what he remembered of the older man, he was often grumpy. But he seemed happier now.

Tanner folded his arms over his chest as the music group began another song. It was unknown to him, and he felt a moment of irritation. He had hoped to find some comfort in the familiarity of the church service. He focused on the words of the song the group was singing, flashed on a screen at the front.

"My refuge, my fortress, my deep sanctuary. My God, my father, through all eternity." Tanner let the words wash over him, realizing that of all the relationships in his life, all the changes and losses, God had always been there, waiting.

Forgive me, Lord, he prayed, and made himself concentrate on the service. The group was finished playing, and Pastor Muller, a man with a beaming smile, came to the front. He looked over the congregation and welcomed everyone, then encouraged the congregation to welcome the people around them with a handshake and a smile.

Tanner turned to Nate first and got a wry smile and a firm handshake.

"Tanner Fortier, how wonderful to see you here," Debbie Suboda, a middle-aged woman sitting with her husband, Mike, in front of him, said, clasping his hand with both of hers. "We missed you."

"Probably because I don't live here anymore," Tanner said.

Debbie's smile slipped as if she understood why that was, but she recovered quickly and patted him on the arm. "That's too bad, of course." Her eyes darted over to Keira in silent question, but Tanner wasn't drawn in. He looked behind him, but no one was sitting there, and then he had nowhere else to turn but to Keira. Should he hold out his hand? He was the guest. Should he welcome her, or should he wait for her to talk?

Instead, he simply nodded at her and went with, "Hello, Keira."

Her response was a tight nod. "Welcome to the service," she said, then looked straight ahead.

He looked at her a moment longer, fighting the same urge he'd felt every time he'd seen her the past couple of days. The urge to demand answers to questions that had tormented him for the past two years. Why hadn't she been willing to talk to him? Why had she ignored his phone calls?

Why had she just left without telling him anything? Explaining anything?

But from the determined set of her jaw and the quick frown thrown his way from Brooke, he knew he wouldn't be getting any answers soon.

He pulled in a long breath and hoped that George Bamford would be able to talk his buddy into letting Tanner stay at his place while he was here.

Refuge Ranch was certainly no refuge for him.

"I CAN'T STAY LONG," Keira said to Brooke, as she glanced at the oversized clock hanging on the wall of the Grill and Chill behind her friend. "Alice said she wanted to visit a friend today and I promised I would make sure Mom had company."

Brooke owned a hairdressing shop in town and though she and Keira saw each other regularly, Brooke had suggested they meet up for coffee this Monday afternoon. Freya was supposed to join them, but she was working over her lunch hour.

But Keira's hopes for some quiet time was ruined the moment they stepped inside the bustling café. The tables were filled with chattering hockey moms and dads full of excitement for the game they had just played.

"So, what happened to your hand?" Brooke asked, pointing to the bandages that Keira still wore.

"Cut myself doing dishes the other day," Keira replied, feeling her cheeks flush as she relived the moment when Tanner bandaged up her finger.

Brooke leaned forward, her brown eyes bright with expectation as she toyed with the purple streak she had put in her hair a few days ago. "So? Tanner? How's that going for you? Is it hard to see him again? Has he missed you?"

She paused to let the barrage of questions linger, as if hoping Keira would answer one of them.

"So? George?" Keira parried, referencing the thirty-five-year-old bachelor owner of the Grill and Chill, who had held Brooke's heart for many years. Unfortunately, Brooke didn't hold George's, a matter that had caused Brooke endless indecision.

"You and Tanner were engaged. You have history," Brooke said, implying that she and George had far less than that. "You haven't seen him since you left Aspen Valley. It's got to be hard to see him now."

"He's part of my past. I've got my future to think of."

"I saw how Tanner looked at you in church," Brooke continued. "I think he still likes you."

Keira clenched her fists against a sudden and unexpected pain. "Please, Brooke, can we stop talking about Tanner?" she asked, keeping her voice quiet, her tone neutral.

Brooke sighed and nodded, then glanced past Keira, her face lighting up. "Oh, my. Here he is."

Groaning, Keira closed her eyes and prayed for strength, for patience, and for the next few days to fly past.

Keira knew the moment Tanner stopped by their table. She had no choice but to look up at him. His head was bare; he tapped his worn cowboy hat against his leg. His cheeks still shone from his shave this morning and she saw a tiny nick on his chin. His white shirt was wrinkled but his blue jeans were brand-new. His gaze landed on Keira, his smile as forced as hers, the tension between them thick as syrup.

"Good to see you again, Tanner," Keira said in a falsely cheerful voice. "How did you like our pastor yesterday?" It was a weird question, but it was the first topic her scattered brain latched onto.

"He's good," Tanner said, turning his attention to Brooke. "I appreciated his message and how he delivered it."

Keira experienced a stab of jealousy at how his smile softened and grew more genuine when he looked at Brooke but tamped it as quickly as it came. She couldn't allow herself to want or need anything from Tanner.

"And I hear you're going to the NFR," Brooke continued, switching topics with lightning speed, obviously ignoring Keira's faint nudges against her leg.

"Yeah. I had a good year."

"So, what brings you to the Grill and Chill?" Keira finally asked, knowing her silence was creating a continued awkwardness.

"George here said he could hook me up with a friend who has a place to stay."

Keira felt relief, with a surprising touch of regret.

"That's good," Keira said with false heartiness. "I hope you find a place to stay."

"I thought you were staying at the Bannisters'?" Brooke asked.

Tanner's eyes slid from Keira's back to Brooke. "It's just easier if I don't. Alice is there already, and I don't want to be a burden to anyone."

"A burden," Brooke scoffed. "Refuge Ranch was like your second home. Though I can see why you wouldn't hang around Alice. Can't believe she didn't change things up so you and Roger could run the ranch together."

This netted her another nudge from Keira, which Brooke also ignored.

"Have you thought about hiring a lawyer?" she continued. "I heard Aria Waldren is really good. Freya works for her and thinks she's amazing."

Another nudge. It was as though her friend was poking a stick around in a bear's den, determined to get a reaction from Tanner. Brooke knew as much about the history of Tanner and his stepmother as Keira did. Why was she pushing?

"It is what it is," Tanner said quietly. "I can't spend too much time looking back over my shoulder. I have to look ahead."

Keira heard an underlying tone in his voice and knew that in some oblique way he was referring to their old relationship.

"Are Monty and John still leaving today?" Tanner asked, glancing at Keira. "I offered to help load the heifers, but they said they would be okay."

"I think that's the plan," Keira said. "Though Dad said he wanted to get some more work done on the saddle this morning before he left, which is why he didn't come to church."

"When will Monty be back?"

She knew he was thinking about his saddle. "They're staying at Giesbrooks' tonight and coming back tomorrow."

He nodded. "So will he get the saddle done on time, you think?"

"If he gets at it as soon as he comes back. How long can you stay?" Obviously, this was very important to him.

"I wanted to head back before Thursday."

She felt a touch of relief. It was hard enough that Lee and Heather weren't coming for Ellen's birthday, having Tanner around would make the celebration that much harder.

"Hey, Tanner. What ill wind blew your restless self into town today?" George Bamford joined them, wiping his hands on a towel, his dark brown eyes flicking over the group. George was tall, lanky, and favored plaid shirts, khaki pants, and sneakers. He'd moved to Aspen Valley ten years ago, bought the Grill and Chill and had been cooking up hamburgers and fries ever since.

"Nor'wester," Tanner quipped.

"Nasty one. Though I hear there's a storm coming in from the north. Another one of those Arctic clippers that never bring anything good."

"There's always a storm brewing in Alberta in the winter," Tanner returned. "So, you find a place for me to stay?"

George's eyes slid to Keira, the faintest question in them as if wondering if it was her fault that Tanner didn't want to stay at Refuge Ranch.

Keira picked up her mug and took another sip of the coffee that had lost any hint of warmth just to avoid George's gaze, Brooke's questions, and Tanner's presence.

"I did. Buddy of mine has a place you can crash," George said, flipping the towel over his shoulder, his hands resting on his hips. "He's gone now but he'll be back tomorrow for a couple hours. Come to his place at seven in the morning and he can give you the keys. Show you what's what."

"Sounds good."

"You girls need anything more?" George asked, turning his attention back to Keira and Brooke. "You want me to get you a hot cup of coffee, Keira?"

Keira caught her friend's eager look upward, but George wasn't paying attention to her.

Her heart broke for her friend. She wished she could tell her that guys will always disappoint you. That it wasn't worth it, but now was not the time or place.

"I'm okay," Keira replied. "I should get going anyhow." She

reached over to get her purse but before she could open it, Tanner had dropped a handful of bills on the table.

"On me," he said, slipping his wallet in his back pocket.

"No. That's okay," Keira protested. "I can pay for this."

"So can I," Tanner said, laying his hand on hers to stop her.

She recognized his usual response to her oft-spoken protest. And for the same slow second, she felt the warmth of his hand on hers. The old rhythms of their old relationship.

Her thoughts slipped, unwanted, back to that moment when he had helped her bandage her hand. The feel of his hand so familiar it created an ache deep in her soul. A yearning for what could never be.

Then he snatched his hand back and Keira felt her chest crumple.

It was a good thing he wasn't staying at the ranch anymore after tomorrow. Seeing him every day was too much a reminder of what she had lost.

CHAPTER FOUR

The sound of a blustering wind howling around the bunkhouse pulled Tanner out of a troubled dream. He groaned, the fresh injury aching as he rolled over onto his back, sleep getting slowly pulled away.

He lazily rolled his head to the side to check the time. The clock radio beside the bed blinked eight-thirty. As the numbers registered, he sat up and tossed the tangled sheets aside.

Too late. He was supposed to have been out of here before seven o'clock to meet George's buddy in town.

He jumped out of bed, shivering as the chill of the bedroom hit him. The woodstove must have gone out last night. Snow ticked at the window as the wind gusted. Sounded like a bad storm out there.

He rotated his shoulder, massaging the pain away, then tugged on his clothes and boots, the cold in the room and the late hour urging him on.

Tanner shivered again as he stripped the bed and folded up the bedding to bring to the house. He'd get some clean sheets, bring them back, make the bed, pack up his stuff and leave.

Again.

He should have known that coming back here had been a mistake. Expecting that Keira would open up to him now, despite years of silence, was dumb optimism drowning out his common sense. If it weren't for the fact that Monty had already taken apart Roger's saddle yesterday and started working on it, Tanner would turn his back on Refuge Ranch for good.

He put his coat on, turned up the collar, dropped his hat on his head and stepped out onto the deck.

Snow slapped his face, and he hunched his shoulders against the howling wind, plowing his way through knee-high snow gathering on the sidewalk. He tried to look down the driveway, but the driving snow decreased visibility.

By the time he got to the house, ice stuck to his eyebrows and slipped down his neck. He opened the door to the house and a gust of wind almost tore it from his hand.

As he stepped inside the porch, the door fell shut behind him and he was immediately enveloped in warmth. He set his bedding on a bench, pulled his hat off and slapped it against his thigh. He brushed what snow he could off his jacket, hung it up, toed off his boots and walked toward the murmur of voices from the dining room.

Ellen and his stepmother sat at the table, a little girl between them.

The toddler was shoving pieces of toast in her mouth, smearing half of it over her chubby cheeks and into the golden curls that framed her round face.

Ellen looked up and smiled at him when he came into the room. "Good morning, Tanner."

She caught the direction of his gaze and smoothed her hand over the little girl's head. "This is Adana, John's daughter. Would you like to join us for breakfast?"

Tanner smiled at the little girl, who was engrossed in her food. "No. Thanks. I should have been gone an hour ago." His gaze ticked over his stepmother, whose attention seemed taken up by buttering some more toast for Adana.

"Pwease. More," Adana asked, now distracted by the egg his mother was mashing up for her.

"Where are you going in this horrible weather?" Ellen asked.

"I've imposed enough. I've found a place I can stay until the saddle is done."

"But you can stay on the ranch," Ellen protested. "You don't have to go."

"I just feel better staying somewhere else. I'll be back to check on the saddle," he said, glancing over at his stepmother. "And I won't leave without saying goodbye."

Alice looked up at him, her smile tight, her eyes glinting behind the dark frames of her glasses. "That's good to know. We'll be watching your performance when you get to Vegas," she said.

Tanner held her gaze a beat longer, thankful for the small moment of connection and acknowledgment. If he won at Vegas or even placed, maybe things would change between them. Maybe that would help him lose that burden of guilt he'd been carrying around the past two years.

Ease the tension between them.

"And I hear you're having a birthday party," Tanner added, turning back to Ellen.

"You won't be here for that?" Ellen asked, the disappointment in her voice making him feel wanted. "You know you're welcome to join us. Lee and Heather can't come—" She stopped, and Tanner easily heard the pain of disappointment with her other two children.

"I appreciate that, but I have to spend some time at the shop in Lethbridge. After all, that pays the bills as much as rodeoing does."

"Of course. I understand."

Tanner caught Ellen's surreptitious gaze at Alice and caught

47

her faint frown. For a moment he wondered what they thought
of the situation. They had never said anything to him, but of
course, they didn't know until after he and Keira had broken up.
By then, he wasn't around at all.

Then Ellen turned back to him, her smile back.

"When you say goodbye to Keira, could you tell her there's a
message from one of her supply companies?" Ellen asked. "They
need to talk to her about an order."

He had figured on simply leaving. But he couldn't say no to
Ellen.

"Okay. I can do that," he said. "Thanks again for your hospi-
tality. And I'll see you in a few days. Bye, Adana," he said to the
little girl, but she was busy eating.

He was losing his touch, he thought as he left the room. Only
one out of the three seemed to be happy to see him, and he
didn't figure he'd do much better with Keira.

Fifteen minutes later, after getting clean sheets and changing
the bed, he was wading through knee-deep drifts to the shop,
his heart sinking with every step. The longer he spent here, the
worse the roads would get.

Keira was bent over her worktable, laying patterns on
leather, when he came into the shop, bringing in a blast of cold
air and a skiff of snow. He saw his saddle pushed off to one side
of the bench. Obviously not a priority for her. He stifled his
frustration and pasted a grin on his face as Keira looked up
from her work.

"Nasty out there," he said with a strained joviality as he
pulled his ice-encrusted hat off, bending down to pat Sugar.
"Thought I'd let you know I'm heading out to Aspen Valley now.
Your mom asked me to let you know that there's a message for
you from some supply place."

Keira nodded. "Thank you."

The silence that followed her terse reply was heavy and
weighted with unspoken questions, but he knew he wasn't

getting anything from her. Which only underlined the reason for him to leave.

So he gave her a tight nod, shoved the door open and then left.

As he got into his truck, he looked at the house, its lights barely discernible through the driving snow. He thought of Ellen in her neck brace. What if something happened to her? What if the driveway got snowed in?

John and Monty were both gone.

Could he in all good conscience leave them all here?

He rested his gloved hands on the wheel of his truck, staring at the snow slanting sideways across the yard, his practical nature fighting with his emotions.

He turned the engine off. He couldn't go. He wouldn't feel right leaving three women and a baby here. Alone in the storm.

Then his cell phone rang. He glanced at the name and number. Monty.

"How are things at the ranch?" Monty asked as soon as Tanner answered.

"Snow's coming down like crazy," Tanner said, wiping the fog from the inside of his windshield. "It looks like a bad storm."

"Here, too. Fact is, we're stuck in the Crowsnest pass." Monty's voice cut in and out and Tanner suspected the storm was creating the poor reception. "Weather reports say that the highway through the area is closed. Are you guys okay there?"

"Yeah. We're fine." Tanner stifled a heavy sigh. Looked as though he wasn't going anywhere today.

"I feel horrible leaving Ellen alone, and John is worried about Adana, but this storm is worse than they forecasted. I'm so glad you're there. Makes both me and John feel more at ease."

"It'll be okay," he said, pushing down his own guilt at his own thoughts of leaving. "Anything that needs to be done today?"

"Cows will need feed. Probably could use some fresh bedding in this snow. Keira was going to do that for me today, anyway, so I'd appreciate it if you could help her. She knows where to put the feed and how much they need. Use the Massey. It's better in the snow."

"Sure thing. Don't rush back."

"We're not going anywhere until the plow trucks get the road cleared. John is texting Alice to let her know what to do about Adana. If the power goes, the generator is ready to go, too. I gassed it up before I left."

"Okay. We'll stay in touch." Tanner said goodbye, then ended the call.

Okay, Lord, like it or not. I guess this is where I'm supposed to be.

He got out, pulled his coat up, and was about to walk over to the shop when he saw Keira coming out, Sugar right on her heels. She was bundled up, hat pulled low over her ears. She was pulling mittens on her hands when she looked up, surprised.

"Just got a call from your father," he called out as he came closer. "He asked me to stay and help out."

Wasn't hard to see the dismay on her face.

"He also asked me to help you feed the cows later," he continued as he stopped in front of her.

"I was just heading out to do that," she protested. "I'm okay to do it myself. You can leave."

"No. I can't. Your dad called and told me the road through the pass is closed. Which means I'm not goin' anywhere. Not until the plow trucks come."

Keira gaped at him, looking like a prisoner who had lost the reprieve she thought she had been granted.

KEIRA STEPPED into the cab of the tractor just as Tanner pulled open the overhead door of the shop the tractor was parked in, letting light and swirling snow come inside.

She closed the door of the tractor's cab and pulled in a long, shaky breath, looking straight ahead. She wanted to pray but right now she was angry with God. For sending the storm. And keeping Tanner here. She felt pushed into a hard, uncomfortable spot. Between a rock and a harder rock, as her father liked to say.

Who was also part of the problem, she fretted as she adjusted the seat of the tractor to move it closer to the controls. Had her dad not invited Tanner to stay, he wouldn't still be here with his smoldering good looks and memories.

She twisted the key halfway, waited for the glow plug light to go off and then turned the key a final turn. Thankfully the tractor started with a roar and a plume of black smoke coming out of the exhaust. Then settled into a deep rumbling as she slowly backed it out of the shop and into the blinding white of the snowstorm.

Tanner stood by the door, Sugar there beside him, tail wagging with expectation as Tanner lowered the door shut behind her. She opened the door and leaned out.

"You may as well come in the cab with me," Keira called out above the wind, squinting toward Tanner.

"I'm okay."

"Don't be an idiot. It's getting colder all the time and those boots aren't exactly made for this snow," she said, pointing to the cowboy boots he still wore.

Tanner looked as though he were about to protest again.

"I'll even let you drive," she said, forcing a grin.

His returning smile was just as forced. Not hard to see he was as uncomfortable around her as she was around him. They would just have to make the best of a bad situation, she thought as he clambered up the metal steps into the tractor. Because from the way the snow was coming down, that situation wasn't changing in the next day or so.

She got out of the seat and wedged herself in the cramped space behind it, hanging on to a handle built into the wall. The cab wasn't small but as soon as Tanner stepped inside, it became suddenly cramped and tight.

He closed the door, put the tractor into gear and slowly backed away.

"The throttle sticks sometimes," Keira said above the roar of the engine, shifting her weight as Tanner engaged the gears. He pressed down, the tractor jerked, and she fell forward.

Her hand automatically came up, catching his shoulder to steady herself. A casual gesture. Something she had done numerous times when she had ridden with him.

It was the solidity of him that made her heart falter. The reality of her hand resting on Tanner's shoulder. Something she hadn't done in many, many years. Something that was so ordinary and now, so foreign.

She snatched her hand back, wishing she could still the sudden racing of her heart.

Tanner didn't even look back. Thankfully he hadn't seemed to notice, or he was just ignoring her. She took a deep breath, dismissing her reaction.

The tractor churned through the snow and headed toward the piled-up hay bales. Tanner easily picked up two bales, nudging them with forks to get the snow off. Keira climbed out of the tractor to open the gate, then got back in after he drove through. The cows, alerted by the noise of the tractor, were already gathered around the feeder. Tanner inched past them, dumped the bales, but just before he got out of the cab of the tractor, he leaned sideways and fished a jackknife out of the pocket of his blue jeans.

Keira's heart jumped as she recognized the wooden handle and the engraving on it.

To Tanner. From Keira.

He caught her looking at the knife and flipped it around. "It's a good knife," he said, his words almost lost in the bawling of the cows and the rumble of the tractor engine.

"Lee helped me pick it out," she said, her mind racing back to that much happier time in her and Lee's life. Before the car accident that put her brother in jail, and before she and Tanner started fighting about his constant rodeoing over the summer.

"Yeah, well. It holds an edge better than any of the other knives I ever had. Be a shame to throw it away."

His dismissive tone pushed down the faint hopes the sight of the knife kindled in her soul. Why had she allowed herself to feel even the slightest bit of hope? She was a fool. Tanner wasn't the man she had once dated, nor was she the woman he was once engaged to. Time and experience had hardened both of them.

Then he opened the door of the tractor, and all conversation was lost.

But as they scrambled over the bales in the feeder, each flick of his jackknife was like a pinprick to her soul.

CHAPTER FIVE

"*A*gain, thanks for dinner," Tanner said as he wiped his mouth. "It was delicious, Alice."

His stepmother gave him a polite smile and nod of acknowledgment across the long, wide table of the Bannisters' dining room. He knew she would have preferred he address her as Mother, but his own father had, for reasons only known to him, encouraged Tanner to call her Alice. And he always had.

The lights above the table flickered, a reminder of the storm still howling outside. Inside, however, a fire crackled in the woodstove, exuding warmth and comfort.

"I've always loved your mother's chicken, Tanner," Ellen said carefully as she placed extra emphasis on the word *mother*.

"I actually got the recipe from you, Keira." Alice glanced at Keira, her smile holding a hint of sorrow. "I remember Roger coming home from having supper here and raving about this amazing chicken recipe that you had made."

Keira's only response was a polite smile. Tanner rubbed his fingers over his temples, wishing this tension would go away. He was probably stuck here another couple of days, he just had to find a way to deal with it.

He'd called the shop in Lethbridge to tell the guys the news, only to find out that the big job they thought they had gotten had been canceled. Right now, stuck out here, it seemed a blessing. It meant that he wasn't immediately needed back there.

His gaze drifted over to Keira, who was carefully scooping another spoonful of mashed potatoes mixed with vegetables for Adana. The little girl was leaning forward in anticipation of the next bite.

"She's a good eater," Ellen said.

"I'm surprised," Tanner said. "That hay we fed the cows this afternoon looks more appealing than that stuff."

"Thanks so much for helping Keira with the cows," Ellen said with a bright smile. "I'm sure the job went a lot faster with the two of you working together."

"Like old times," Tanner said dryly.

"And you even got some work done in the shop?" Ellen asked Keira, pushing past the awkwardness that hung like a cloud over the table.

"Not as much as I'd hoped, but if work goes well, I should have all my orders done by tomorrow," Keira said.

"Did you get some more work done on Roger's saddle?" Alice asked.

"No. I...I was thinking I might work on it tonight."

"Don't do that—"

"No. You can't—"

Tanner and Ellen spoke at the same time, then Ellen held up her hand. "Sorry, Tanner, you were saying?"

"I was just thinking that the storm is still blowing hard. Maybe not such a good idea to go out in the dark."

"I can find my way to the shop," Keira replied to Tanner, but she was looking at her mother.

"Will you be able to get the saddle done on time if you don't work on it tonight?" Alice asked.

Tanner wished she would stop putting extra pressure on

Keira, though he knew he was just as guilty. He wanted the saddle done, as well, but not if it meant Keira had to go out in a howling storm after sunset. Alberta's history was littered with stories of ranchers heading out to their barns in such storms and losing their way back to their houses less than a hundred feet away.

"I'll have time tomorrow. We probably don't have to feed the cows," Keira said, still not looking at either him or Alice.

"I remember how proud Roger was of that saddle," Alice said. "He always told me that he sat better on the horse knowing he was using a saddle from one of the best saddle makers in the business. Of course, as far as I'm concerned, it doesn't matter what you're sitting on when you're on a huge, out of control bronc." She added a light laugh and was joined by Ellen.

"I'm sure you know how that goes," Ellen said to Tanner, pulling him into the conversation.

"I do," he said. "I've drawn some tough horses. So did Roger. We were always competing, though."

Alice gave him a careful smile. "Roger always looked up to you, you know."

Tanner wasn't sure about that, but he let it go. "I still catch myself looking up from the chute, expecting to see him there, helping me get ready," Tanner said.

He caught Alice's warm gaze, realizing that he had said exactly the right thing. Inspired by the benevolence he caught in her eyes, he launched into a story about a particularly good run he and Roger had had at a rodeo at Fort Worth. They had both finished high up in the standings.

"That was a good week," Tanner said with a pensive tone. "I miss him. A lot. There's not much a person can count on in this world, but I could always count on Roger."

Keira stood suddenly, plucking Adana from her chair. "I should give this little munchkin a bath," she said, then without a backward glance, left the room.

Tanner frowned at her unexpected departure, wondering what had triggered it.

Probably my continuing presence, he thought, standing up himself.

"May as well get these dishes cleared off," he said, stacking the plates. Alice joined him, telling Ellen to go sit in the living room.

But while he and Alice were working, he could hear Keira in the bathroom, talking with Adana, singing to her, laughing. The opposite of the woman who had sat in stony silence across the table from him.

Lord, how did we end up here? he prayed as he rinsed and sorted dishes. *How am I going to get through the next few days?*

He didn't get an answer, but he hadn't really been expecting one. It was simply the cry of his lonely heart.

At least he and Alice seemed to be on better terms. As they did the dishes, they chatted and shared stories about Roger, which seemed to bring them closer. At least that was one positive result from being stranded on the ranch.

When they were done, he and Alice joined Keira and Ellen in the living room. He started when he saw Keira with Adana on her lap, turning pages of a worn board book. Keira was reading quietly, her voice animated. Tanner watched her, so relaxed with that little girl. So natural.

She would make a good mother.

The thought caught him short. If things had gone the way he'd planned, he and Keira might have had a child or two by now.

He shook the thought off, jumped to his feet and grabbed a log to throw onto the fire.

"I am so thankful Monty hauled in enough wood to hold us for a couple of days," Ellen said, settling back in her chair as the lights flickered again. "At least we'll be able to stay warm if the power goes out."

"Monty told me the generator was ready to go," Tanner assured her. "We'll be okay."

"I have to say I'm thankful you're here," Ellen said as Keira set a squirming Adana on the floor.

They sat a moment in silence that felt, to Tanner, as strained as it had before.

"Well, I'm tired," Alice said with a sad smile. "Keira, do you mind helping your mother get ready for bed?"

"Of course not. I'm going to put this munchkin to bed, too," Keira said, picking Adana up from the mess of books and DVD cases she had created.

Ellen got up and walked toward the bookcase, slowly crouching down to pick up the books and cases that Adana had spilled.

"Here, let me help you with that," Tanner said, hurrying over to her.

"It's okay. I need to feel like I can do something," she said with a groan as she reached over and picked up a DVD case. She looked down at it as she struggled to her feet. "Oh, look at this. An old DVD that Monty made," she said suddenly.

"You still have DVDs?" Tanner teased.

"You know Monty. He can't throw anything away." Ellen turned it over, looking puzzled. "I wonder what's on this one?" She walked slowly over to the television.

While Tanner tidied up the books and the cases, guessing as to where they were supposed to go, Ellen turned on the television and the DVD player and put the disc inside. As the picture came on, Tanner heard wind and some laughter. He finished putting the books away, then, curious, got up to see what Ellen was playing.

All he saw was an empty corral, the barns, and then off camera, he heard the whinny of a horse. The camera wobbled as Monty, obviously the one filming, encouraged someone to bring the horse around.

Then the camera moved, catching two figures doubled up, riding the horse bareback, and Tanner's heart plunged.

Keira sat in the front, holding the reins. Tanner sat behind her. Her head rested on his chest, and he had his arms wrapped around her waist, his head tucked against hers.

They were both laughing. Carefree. Happy.

"Look at you two," Ellen said, sorrow edging her voice. "You were so in love back then."

Such an innocent time, Tanner thought. Before his father's death when he still foolishly thought he would someday get part ownership of the ranch. When he thought he had enough to offer Keira, daughter of one of the biggest ranchers in the county.

"My goodness that was a while ago," Ellen was saying as she slowly lowered herself into the chair behind her.

On the television, Keira was laughing, the wind tossing her hair around. She caught it in her right hand and Tanner caught the glint of the diamond on her slender finger.

"You're blinding me with that rock," Monty teased, off camera. "How about a kiss from the newly engaged lovebirds?"

Keira laughed again but then leaned her head back and his head lowered, capturing her lips in a kiss even as he covered their faces with his cowboy hat.

The camera shook, as Monty laughed. "No need to be shy," he called out.

As he watched, Tanner's heart turned over, and he wished he could look away.

Suddenly Keira entered the room, still carrying a book. "Well, she's all settled in for the night, I—"

She came to a dead stop. The book slid out of her fingers, falling with a thud on the floor as she stared at the television screen.

"What is this?"

"An old video I found of you and Tanner trying out that

mare that your father was convinced would be the foundation of his new horse herd," Ellen said, turning awkwardly around to look at her daughter.

"Turn that off," Keira said, her voice a strangled sound.

"Pardon me, honey?" Ellen asked.

"Please. Turn it off," she repeated.

"But sweetheart—"

Then without a word of explanation, Keira fled the room, running up the stairs. Retreating.

Tanner fought the urge to follow her. To ask her what was going on.

Instead, he walked over to the bookshelf on the pretense of fixing up the books there as he heard the door of her bedroom slam.

He sighed, stifling his reactions. Talking to Keira was a waste of time. He knew he would get no answers from her tonight. Maybe never.

THE SEWING MACHINE CLUNKED, then stuck.

Keira yanked the leather out of the machine, turned it over and groaned at the snarl of threads at the bottom of the piece. It would take her forever to snip and cut and then untangle everything from the bobbin of the sewing machine, and in ten minutes Tanner was coming to get her to feed the cows. He had offered to do it himself, but it was too big a job for one person in this weather.

She shivered, wishing she had started a fire this morning instead of relying on the small electric heater in the corner of the shop that barely kept the cold at bay.

She blew on her fingers, drew in a long breath and grabbed her scissors and snipped at the threads, wishing she could as easily excise the images from the movie she had seen last night.

Her and Tanner.

Him kissing her.

Their utter and complete happiness.

Keira snipped too forcefully and jabbed herself in the finger, right beside the cut that she had sustained when she and Tanner had done dishes. In a fit of anger, she tossed the scissors aside and pushed herself away from the machine. This was ridiculous. In the past few years, she'd found her balance and had found, if not happiness, at least a measure of contentment. Now she felt tossed and turned. Battered and worn down.

She pounded her fists on the table in front of her, fighting her anger and frustration.

And, even worse, the lingering appeal his presence created.

Remnants of old feelings flitted through her mind, creating a frustrating mixture of dread and anticipation at the thought of seeing Tanner again.

Lord, I don't know why I'm dealing with this right now, she prayed, staring straight ahead. *But I'm tired of it. I want it gone.*

She drew in a long, slow breath, realizing her prayer was more of a demand than a supplication.

You know what you need to do.

The words slunk around at the edges of her mind, taunting her.

No. That wasn't necessary. She'd spent the past few years burying the past. No sense resurrecting it now. It would serve no purpose.

She couldn't bear it.

Then the door of the shop opened, bringing in a gust of cold air. Sugar trotted in, and after her came Tanner, snow covering his hat and shoulders. The snow was still coming down, harder than before.

"Hey, there," he said. "I've got the tractor running." He glanced at the piece of leather still stuck in the sewing machine. "I can do it on my own if you have work to do."

"It's too cold to do it on your own," she said, walking over to the hooks that held her winter clothes. She tugged on her toque, then grabbed her snow pants and coat, beginning the painstaking work of layering for the weather outside. As she pulled her scarf off the hook, she caught Tanner's wry smile.

"You've completely disappeared under all that stuff."

"I hate being cold," she said as she proceeded to wrap her scarf around her neck, but her bulky coat made it difficult for her to reach behind her head and her scarf got tangled up in her toque, pulling it off her head. She grabbed her hat, tugged it on and tried again but the scarf tangled up in the hood of her oilskin coat.

"Let me help you." And before she could protest, he straightened it, then wound it carefully around her neck.

He stood so close she could smell the scent of soap and his aftershave, a smell so familiar it created a dull ache in her chest. She had to fight the impulse to drift toward him. Lean into him like she did so often when she was younger. Like she had on the video.

She pulled away, concentrating on tucking the ends of her scarf in her coat, determined not to let him get to her. Then her gaze drifted up and caught him watching her, a question lingering in his eyes.

She was about to push past him when he caught her by the arm.

"I want to ask you a question," he said.

Which was exactly what she was trying to avoid.

"Why did that video make you so upset?" he continued.

Her first reaction was anger, but behind that came the usual guilt.

"It reminded me of happier times," was all she managed to squeak out.

He was quiet a moment, then narrowed his eyes. "Why would that bother you so much? *You* were the one who broke up with me. *You* were the one who took off without answering my calls."

He had to raise his voice above the wind howling around the building to make himself heard and it put her on the defensive.

"You knew exactly why I took off," she returned. "We fought enough about it. You were gone all the time with your work and the rodeo."

"That's old ground. When I came back from the rodeo, after we broke up, I tried to call you. I wanted to try again. To figure out how we could make it work. But you didn't return any of my calls. Don't you think I at least deserved a second chance? You took off without even acknowledging that. Didn't I at least deserve a reason?" His voice deepened and grew harsher as he took a step toward her.

Keira couldn't help herself. She moved back, holding up one hand to stop him.

He seemed confounded by her reaction.

"See, we're fighting again," she said, trying to maintain a physical and emotional distance between them. "And we're fighting about the same things we fought about then. It was pointless for us to try again because we would have been doing this. Going in circles around the same old stuff." She stopped there, her voice choking off. Her explanation sounded lame, even to her own ears, but it was all she could give him right now.

She could tell he didn't believe her, but thankfully he didn't seem to press the point.

"You're right. I'm sorry." He drew in a deep breath, then gave her a cautious smile. "I don't want to fight. I just...I just want some explanation. Some resolution."

It was the hurt in his voice that made her realize she had to give him more than the vague comments she always had. She hadn't just walked away from a boyfriend wanting to make up. She had walked away from a fiancé. They had made a commitment to each other. Trouble was, the fact that he had wanted to try again after she had broken up with him had come as too little too late.

"I'm sorry I didn't at least return your calls. I...I overreacted to a situation."

"What situation? Me being gone?"

She latched onto that.

"That was part of it." She could tell by the frustration on his face that she had given him precisely zero. "There's more..." Her voice trailed off as she tried to weigh what to tell him.

He nodded his head slowly, as if absorbing this information. "Am I going to get that 'more' now?"

"I don't know."

Tanner looked up at the roof as a particularly strong gust of wind rattled the tin, then back at her. "From the sounds of the storm I'm not going anywhere soon."

Keira wasn't comforted by the quiet persistence in his voice. She knew from their past that she had given him enough leeway that he would push until he got what he thought he needed.

"Before we go feed cows, I need to tell you something, too." He held her gaze, his eyes piercing hers. "Like you said, we fought a lot, but I want you to know why I was working so much back then."

Her mind slipped back to those horrible days when it seemed like every time she and Tanner got together he was tired or cranky. "You said you wanted to have enough set by."

He had said it so often, she had thought it was an excuse. Which was another reason they fought.

"There was another reason."

"Your father's will?"

"Yes."

His single word response gave her the courage to carry on this much safer line of conversation.

"Why didn't you tell me that was why you were working so

hard? I had to find out from Roger what Alice told you." The fact that Tanner hadn't told her himself hurt almost as much as their fighting had.

So much could have been so different had he only told her right away.

"I didn't tell you because I was too proud," he said, his voice holding an edge that showed her how much it still bothered him and how hard it was for him to say this. "I didn't want anyone to know that my dad still saw me as second best. That Roger was his priority even though I was in his life longer. I struggled to reconcile the man who I saw as my father with the man who so easily cut me out of his life." He paused there as if gathering his emotions together.

Keira could only stare at him, regret and sorrow spiraling through her.

"So, I figured I had to find another way to give you what you wanted."

"And what was that?"

Tanner set his hands on his hips, his head skewed to one side. "You're a Bannister. Your family has held this ranch for almost a hundred and fifty years. An unbroken legacy of land ownership and expansion. Your parents had never had to watch their expenses."

"I wasn't spoiled," she protested, slapping her mittens against her thigh in disapproval.

"Maybe not, but you could have had anything you wanted. And though I wasn't raised poor, either, I counted on inheriting some of the ranch. It was going to give us a life, a living. When I didn't, I had to find another way to support you. That's why I took on the mechanic job. I would have loved to work in Aspen Valley or somewhere closer, but Lethbridge was the only place I could get work. And that's why I started rodeoing as much as I did. I was trying to save up to give us a good future. So, I could give you what I thought you should have."

"All I ever wanted was you."

The words burst out of her before she could stop them. They hung in the air between them, and Keira knew she had taken a step down a road she couldn't easily retreat from.

"What do you mean?" he asked, his eyes narrowing. "You didn't return any of my calls when I tried to contact you that summer. You couldn't even send me a text message." His accusations battered at her, wearing her down.

"Anything I could have said, we covered in every fight we had after you started working off the ranch," she muttered. "I didn't talk to you after you left because…I didn't…didn't want to fight anymore. We had nothing more to say to each other and you weren't around to talk to."

Tanner rocked back and forth on his heels. "And we're back to that." His words came out in a staccato burst. Like he didn't believe her entirely.

"I guess," was her lame response.

"We're not done with this," Tanner said, his tone quiet. Ominous. "I know there's more to say. I've never been a patient man, but I've learned a lot over the past few years. And right now, I've got time to find out what you're not telling me. I'm not going anywhere until the plow trucks come."

Then he walked away, leaving Keira feeling as if she had woken a sleeping cougar.

CHAPTER SIX

"Do you think the storm will be over soon?" Alice asked when she came back into the living room after putting Ellen to bed. "Your mother's birthday celebration is only two days away."

Tanner heard the anxiety in her voice. Had she thought he would stay around for that?

"I don't know," he said, looking up from the book he'd been pretending to read the past half hour. Keira, sitting on the floor just a few feet away, sorted through a basket of wool. "Unless the storm stops now, I doubt it."

"What should we do?" Alice asked. "We can't have a birthday party without Monty around. Would you mind if we put it off?" she asked, looking at Keira. "Celebrate it next week? Maybe Heather and Lee could come if we did that?"

"That'd be fine with me," Keira said. "It seems kind of point-less to have a celebration like that without Dad, either."

The fire crackled and snapped in the stove, a warm buffer to the storm that had picked up again as the sun set. Tanner tried to keep his attention on his book, but he kept looking over at

Keira, thinking of the frustrating conversation they'd had this afternoon.

He knew there was more going on, but he also knew when to push and when to back off. He'd worked with enough skittish horses to recognize the signs. Keira had been right about one thing. They had fought often and always about the same thing. Maybe she did feel as if there was nothing more to say. Maybe she did feel he wouldn't have listened if she explained to him why she wasn't ready to give him a second chance that summer. He knew he should have told her earlier about his problems with Alice and his inheritance but turned out she knew before he tried to connect with her again.

Which meant something else was going on with her. Something she wasn't telling him. The storm that still blustered outside told him that he might have time to find out what it was.

"And did you get more work done on Roger's saddle?" Alice asked, glancing expectantly from Tanner to Keira.

"I got the swell cover replaced and I hope to finish that tomorrow," Keira replied as she sorted through the bright colors of yarn in the basket in front of her. Apparently, she was knitting a scarf for Adana.

"Will the saddle be done on time?" Alice pressed.

Keira's only response was a tight nod as she set a couple of balls of wool aside.

"The saddle doesn't seem as badly damaged as Keira initially thought," Tanner put in, helping Keira out, wishing his stepmother would stop pressuring her. "We should be able to get it fixed up soon."

"I think it's so wonderful that you're using Roger's saddle," Alice said to Tanner. "I know he was proud of it. Did you two notice the marks in the saddle? Roger said he put a cross on the back of the seat for every top ride he completed in the money."

"Trust Roger to do that," Keira muttered.

"What do you mean?" Tanner asked, puzzled at her comment.

"Just a joke," she said, tugging on a particularly snarly bit of wool that was caught on the edge of the basket.

Only she didn't look like she was joking.

"He had a lot of crosses on that saddle," Alice continued, seemingly unaware of Keira's comment. "Did you notice them, Tanner?"

"Roger had told me about them." Tanner aimlessly flipped through another page of the book. He knew they were there but hadn't pointed them out to Keira. She had been reluctant enough to work on the saddle; he doubted seeing Roger's self-indulgence would have helped.

Another burst of wind and snow told him that the storm had picked up again. He hoped the cows wouldn't bunch up and push the fences. The wires were sound, but hundreds of cows all trying to head away from a storm could push over even the tightest fence.

He glanced over at Keira again, surprised to see her looking at him. But as soon as they made eye contact, she looked away. Just as she had all night.

"Roger had such stories about his trips away from home," Alice murmured, her voice holding a note of sorrow. "I miss listening to them. I remember one he told me about a rodeo clown who used to play practical jokes on him. Did he ever tell you about that, Tanner?"

Tanner looked up from his book. "Can't remember," he said.

"This clown was a girl, which is unusual in the rodeo. Anyhow, she used to play these practical jokes on him. Pepper in his boots and grease in his gloves. That kind of thing. Apparently, Roger was the only one she used to target, which seems somewhat unkind," Alice said.

Tanner wasn't too surprised. Roger could be a pest and didn't always know when to quit.

"Apparently this clown had a broom that she used all the time. It was a main prop of hers," Alice continued, smiling as she remembered. "She would lean on it all the time while she was telling jokes to the crowd. Well, Roger had cut the broom somehow and put it back together so the clown couldn't see. The first time that clown leaned on it she fell face down in the dirt. Of course, everyone else thought it was part of her act, but the clown knew better. After that, Roger and that girl were always finding ways to get back at each other. Got to be a thing with them." Alice chuckled. "I can't believe he didn't tell you that story."

"Actually, I do remember now," Tanner said as he set the book aside, folding his hands over his stomach, a gentle smile teasing his lips. "I remember that he couldn't get her to notice him, which is why, I suspect, he kept playing jokes on her."

"Well, she didn't know what she was missing," Alice said. "Roger was the most charming young man."

Keira released a faint snort, which made him look her way, but she was looking down at the wool she was still untangling. He wondered what that was about.

"I always hoped he would settle down someday," Alice said. "But I also know that he wanted to experience as much as he could before he did. I know you both saw a lot of country in your travels."

"That we did. Made lots of memories." Tanner released a gentle sigh, sorrow filling the moment.

And once again he felt that all-too-familiar crush of guilt followed by its ever-present companion, regret. If only he hadn't let Roger go out on his own.

He glanced over at Alice, only to see her watching him. The sorrow in her eyes made him assume she was thinking the same thing he was.

"He was a good son." Alice sighed lightly, then turned to

Keira. "What about you, Keira? You and Tanner and Roger used to hang around. Do you have any memories to share?"

Keira kept her head down, tugging on a particularly stubborn knot. "None that Tanner doesn't know already."

"But you went to school with him. And there was that summer after Tanner left that you and him—"

"That was a long time ago," Keira said, abruptly interrupting Alice midsentence.

That made Tanner wonder. Did it have some connection to her evasiveness in the shop this afternoon? He was about to ask what was going on when, suddenly, the house was plunged into darkness.

"Just stay put," Tanner said, getting up, letting his eyes adjust to the sudden darkness. After a few moments, he could slowly make out the glow from the woodstove and the outlines of the furniture. "Keira, where are the flashlights?"

"I'll get them," she said, rising slowly to her feet, an indistinct silhouette.

"Just tell me where they are," he insisted.

"No. It's easier for me to find them," she snapped, fear edging her voice.

Her angry response surprised him. She had never been afraid of the dark before.

His eyes slowly adjusted, and he saw Keira bending over the side table by the couch. She yanked open the drawer and rummaged through it, as if she wasn't sure what she was looking for.

"Here we are," she said, her voice breathless, relieved.

Tanner heard the click of a button and a beam of light flashed into the darkness, wavering as it illuminated the living room and kitchen.

"Do you have another one?" Tanner asked.

"Take this one. I'll get the other one out of the kitchen drawer."

Her hand was ice-cold, and it trembled when she handed him the flashlight.

"Are you okay?" Tanner asked quietly, her face a white mask in the glow of the light, her eyes wide with what looked like fear.

"Yeah. I'm fine," she said with a forced smile.

"Where are your candles?" Alice asked. "I can light them if you have them."

"I'll get you the battery-powered lantern from the kitchen," Keira said, turning around. Tanner followed her, shining the flashlight onto the floor where she walked. She retrieved the lantern and another flashlight. They turned on the lantern, sending deep shadows into the room.

"I'll go check on Ellen," Alice said, flicking on her flashlight and leaving.

"And I'll have to start up the generator," Tanner said. They couldn't leave the power off too long. The cattle needed their heated waterers, and lines would freeze if they didn't get auxiliary power up and running.

"Okay. Let's do it, then," Keira said.

"You don't need to come," Tanner protested. "Your dad said it was ready to go." He couldn't understand why she would willingly go out into the storm with him when she had made it clear she preferred to avoid him.

"The generator is fiddly." Keira walked slowly toward the porch, flashlight bobbing. "It'll take two people to get it going."

"Okay. I know I can't stop you if you've got your mind set on something."

Even in the feeble light of the flashlights he caught the annoyance in her face. She was a puzzle these days, that much he knew. A woman with layers of unanswered questions. It was starting to get to him. Keira had always been a straightforward girl. She always said she left the mystery and drama to Heather, her sister.

"Do you have any rope?" he asked as he pulled on his gloves and picked up his flashlight, the beam of light dancing around the porch as gusts of wind buffeted the house.

"In the blanket box," Keira said, pointing her own flashlight toward a large box in one corner of the porch.

"Don't know why your family always called this the blanket box," Tanner muttered as he walked over and opened it. "Far as I remember I've never seen blankets in here."

Keira chuckled at his comment. "I think it was my grandmother's, though I'm not so sure she had blankets in it, either. Heather and I used to hide in it when we played hide-and-seek."

Tanner pulled out a coil of rope, checking it for length. "I remember that. Could never figure out why you girls would want to shut yourselves up in such a cramped spot."

"I stopped hiding there after that time that Roger sat on the lid."

"He did that?"

"Oh, yeah. Seemed forever before he let me out of there. I'll never forget how he was laughing at me. He could be such a jerk." Keira stopped, then released a light laugh, as if it was all in fun. "Sorry. I shouldn't say that about him when he's not here to defend himself."

Jerk was a strong word for Keira, who seemed to get along with everyone.

"It wasn't that bad, was it?" Tanner asked as he coiled up the rope. "We had some fun times together, the three of us."

"Let's get going." Keira clamped her hand on the flashlight, obviously not wanting to talk about Roger anymore.

"I'm tying this rope to the door handle of the house," Tanner said before he opened the door. "And we're hanging on to it no matter what." Even with their flashlights, the snow and darkness would completely disorient them.

She nodded as she pulled her hood up and over her stocking

cap. Tanner tied up one end of the rope with quick, sure movements.

Then, together, clinging to the rope, they headed out into the blinding storm.

"I THINK it's this screw that needs to be tightened," Tanner muttered, bending closer to the generator.

"Phillips, Robertson or flathead?" Keira pulled open her dad's toolbox that was sitting on a small bench inside the generator shed. Thankfully they didn't need their flashlights in here. A battery-powered light, which was triggered to come on when the power went off, was plugged into an outlet inside the shed, giving off a watery glow.

The air inside the shack was bone-deep cold and the sooner they could get this generator going, the quicker they could get back to the warmth of the house.

"Philips," Tanner said. Keira guessed at the size, pulled a couple out and handed him the first one.

"Bingo," he said, fitting it into the screw head and tightening it. He jiggled the starting motor. It looked tight, but now Tanner had to rewind the rope that had come loose when he tried to start it the first time.

"It's not getting any warmer in here, is it?" Keira asked, rubbing her hands together.

"Nope. It isn't." Tanner tugged his gloves off, tucked them inside his coat and slid his bare hands inside as well to warm them up. He looked over at her, and the expression on his face told her that he wasn't done with the conversation they'd had this afternoon in the shop.

"So, Keira, why are you so uncomfortable around my stepmother?"

She hadn't expected this. "What do you mean?"

Tanner hunched his shoulders forward, still holding her gaze with his steady, piercing one. "I know you're not crazy about her, but it's not like you to be so short with her."

Keira rubbed her hands again then tucked them inside her coat, as well, leaning against the wall behind her. "This is hardly the ideal place for a heart-to-heart," she said quietly, her breath making fragile clouds of fog in the pallid light.

"I know."

"And if you recall, you didn't always get along with her, either," Keira countered.

"I know that, too. But since she found out that I'm using Roger's saddle, she seems to have softened toward me. And I don't mind being on her good side for a change. I've spent a lot of my life trying to find that part of her. I'm enjoying it for now."

"Have you forgiven her? For not wanting to let you work the ranch?" Keira took a side trip to another topic, trying to find her way through this conversation.

Tanner's heavy sigh said more than his words ever could. "I guess I had to come to the point that it wasn't her I had to forgive. It was my father. He was the one who made up the will. He was the one who didn't look after me."

"At one time you talked about hiring a lawyer. Did you ever go through with that?" Keira had left before she could find out the outcome of that situation.

"I did hire someone but then…I dropped it." Tanner shifted his stance, his eyes holding hers. "Besides, I had no reason to go after it after Roger died and you and I…" He let the sentence trail off. But she had a niggling suspicion there was more he wasn't telling her.

"Alice is a complex person," Tanner continued. "I can't begin to understand her, but right now she's the only relative I have left, other than a couple of aunts and uncles, who I know even less than I know Alice. I'm kind of glad she's staying here at the ranch right now. Taking care of your mom. It gives me a chance to spend more time with her."

"And I'm thankful she's taking care of my mom, don't get me wrong," Keira admitted. "She's capable and helpful. Though it's been hard to have her around twenty-four seven."

"Why is that?"

Keira felt as if she had to drag the answer from deep inside her. But she knew he wasn't going to leave it alone. "I guess... I know she's your stepmother, but I've always thought she could be nicer to you. I'm sorry, but it's hard to listen to her going on about Roger like he's everything and you're nothing. Roger always will be her favorite."

"He's her natural child. I was the kid she had to take into her life."

"She knew that going into the marriage. And she's known you since you were a little boy. I always hated the way she favored Roger over you again and again." Her words came out harder than she had intended. "And the whole deal with your dad willing the ranch completely to her? I mean, how did that happen? How did she manage to have such a hold on him that he completely bypassed you?"

"I wasn't his biological child," he reminded her.

"But you were his son."

Tanner was quiet, his lips pressed together, thinking of the last, final insult he had discovered a few years after his father's death.

"Well, maybe he thought she would be fair."

"And we all know how that turned out," Keira continued, surprised he was able to say that about Alice. "She made it abundantly clear Roger would be getting the ranch. That was hardly fair." She stopped herself there, remembering Tanner's pain this afternoon when they had talked about his reasons for taking on all the extra work he did after his father died. All so that he could afford, in his mind, to set them up in a style to which he assumed she was accustomed because he couldn't tell her that his original plan of living on the ranch had fallen through.

Once again regret curled through her. If she had known earlier about the will. If he had told her right away…

She looked into his face, his eyes holding hers, she wondered if she could tell him the rest.

"Anyway, that's why I don't like her. She's so obviously favoring Roger, making him out to be such a fun, loving person. And we both know he wasn't."

Tanner frowned at her comment. "What do you mean?"

Keira closed her eyes a moment, the chill from the shack slowly seeping into her bones. She had started this, she had to finish it.

"I'm sure you remember that summer we broke up. When you were gone and Roger was injured?"

"How could I forget? Worst summer of my life."

The pain in his voice made her, once again, bitterly regret their fights. How she had pushed him to stay home more without knowing why he was working so hard. Would she have broken up with him had she known all his reasons?

They would never know.

She hesitated a moment, then plunged ahead. "It was a lousy summer for me, too. I…regretted breaking up with you."

She caught a flash of frustration on his features, knowing that he was probably thinking back to his texts and emails asking her to get back together.

She pushed on. "Anyhow, Roger was injured, and I was lonely, and Roger was antsy, and we spent a lot of time together. We even went out a couple of times."

Tanner's sudden frown made her wish she hadn't said anything, but he deserved to know this much.

"*Out* as in coffee like we used to do all together?"

"No. Out as in a date. We went to a few movies. And some

parties." Her voice broke and she wondered if she could say the words she needed to.

"Was he the reason you broke up with me?" Tanner's eyes narrowed, his voice colder than the storm outside.

"No. Not at all." She pressed her hands together and forced herself to carry on. "This was after we broke up. I realized I made—made a mistake. I know I shouldn't have broken up with you after your father died. I know that now, that you were grieving, but we were fighting all the time. Just like your parents. I didn't want that for us."

She stopped there, knowing she had no right to expect understanding, but they hadn't had a chance to talk this all through.

"But I knew that it would be hard to get back together with you..." She let the sentence drift off, feeling Tanner's anger coming off him in waves.

"So only a couple of weeks after we break up, you're dating my brother?"

Keira pressed her lips together; his eyes glittered like ice chips in his pinched features.

She forced herself to hold his gaze and not back down. "We had broken up."

"So you could go out with Roger? Who would probably be taking over the ranch?"

She sucked in her breath at the suppressed anger in his voice. "You think I went out with him because you were a less appealing prospect?"

"I'm sorry, but that's how it looks from my side."

"Well, you're wrong. I don't know how I can convince you otherwise. And there was no way I broke up with you to date Roger. That just...just happened. It was just a...a temporary stupidity on my part. It meant nothing. Absolutely nothing."

Don't raise your voice. Keep control of your emotions.

Tanner looked up at her, the anger now replaced by a

sadness that bothered her even more. "You said yourself you didn't like the way my mother favored Roger. Don't you think I knew that, too? And now I find out that you dated my stepbrother?"

Keira wrapped her arms around her midsection, hugging herself from the chill that came not only from the outside but also from deep in her soul.

"I'm sorry," she said. "Not one of my better decisions. I realized...realized he wasn't my type."

"Is that why you left Aspen Valley?"

She shivered in the chill of the shack, nodding. "I was ashamed of myself and knew I had made a dumb mistake. Even though we weren't a couple anymore, I didn't think you would appreciate us being together."

"I don't like it now. I can't imagine how I would have felt then." His admission released some of the tension that had been gripping her up till now. "I know I had—have," he corrected, "a bad temper. I guess I can't blame you for not telling me back then."

She relaxed. "I'm sorry. So sorry. Like I said, I wasn't proud of myself. It was one of my dumber decisions, along with breaking up with you. But after...after Roger, I needed to get away from Aspen Valley for a while. I felt like there was nothing here for me. I wanted a new start in a new place."

Tanner gave her a careful smile. "And that's why you never came to Roger's funeral?"

Keira knew this was a sticking point for Tanner. "I had other things going in my life at the time," she said quietly. "Roger and I didn't part on the best of terms. And that's why I didn't return your texts or your phone calls. I felt stupid for going out with Roger and I knew you'd be upset."

He held her gaze, his eyes piercing into her soul.

"I would have been," he admitted. "So, that's why I never heard from you?"

She nodded, pulling in a heavy breath. "I'm sorry," she ventured. "I should have let you know."

"No. I get it." He smiled at her, which she returned.

Then he pushed himself away from the wall, tugged his gloves out of his pocket and pulled them on. "Let's see if we can get this generator going."

She was thankful for his quiet acceptance.

He turned his attention back to the generator. Then gave the starting cord a pull. Nothing. Then again. Nothing. Finally, on the third pull it roared to life, drowning out anything else they might have to say to each other. The regular lights inside the shack blazed to life. Everything seemed to be working all right.

Tanner stood back a moment, waiting to make sure it was still going, then nodded toward the door. Time to go back to the house. Before she stepped out the door she looked back at him, trying to get a read on his mood.

He was smiling again.

And for the first time in a long while a small ray of hope winked to life.

She knew they would probably never be a couple again. But if they could find a way to be friends, that could be enough.

Couldn't it?

CHAPTER SEVEN

"I think I'd like the stirrups pushed back some more," Tanner said, handing Keira the stirrup leathers that she needed to reattach. "If you're putting new ones on anyhow, may as well put them where they work best for me. Just adjust that back bind and the quarter bind for length."

As she took the leathers from him, he held on to them a moment longer to get her attention.

She looked up at him, a question in her eyes.

"I'm glad you told me about Roger," he said quietly, feeling the need to bring everything out into the open in the quiet and privacy of the shop. "That explains a lot for me."

That wasn't entirely true. It still seemed odd to him that her dating Roger was what sent her away from Aspen Valley and kept her from calling him back, but she obviously thought there was no reason to stay.

So why had she come back at all? And after Roger's funeral?

He pushed that question aside. That was in the past. He wanted to move on. Take advantage of the bit of ground he had gained last night with her confession.

Her smile eased some of the tension that had hummed

between them when he first came here. "I'm glad. I didn't like it that we...we weren't getting along. This is nice."

Nice wasn't a word he liked to use when it came to him and Keira, but for now *nice* was better than what had come before. *Nice* was a step down a road he hadn't seen for a long while.

But first he had to get the NFR behind him. Bury the guilt that haunted him since Roger's death.

Then hopefully he and Keira could move on from *nice* to something beyond that.

He walked back to the table, clearing off the scraps of leather that lay there. Remnants of the stirrup leathers they had measured and cut out a few moments ago. He walked over to the garbage can beside the desk and dropped them in while she reinforced the straps with lines of sewing.

Then he saw her Bible lying open on the desk. Curious what she was reading, he picked it up. He skimmed over the passages, trying to find what it was that had given her nourishment. He saw a passage underlined in Isaiah 43, verse 18.

"Forget the former things; do not dwell on the past." *See, I am doing a new thing!* "Now it springs up; do you not perceive it?"

He read the words again, wondering what she'd found in them that made her underline them. Then, as he was about to lay the book back, a piece of pink paper, worn and tattered, fluttered out of the back of her Bible. He glanced over at Keira, feeling as if he had invaded her privacy, but she was bent over the machine, a frown of concentration puckering her forehead, and hadn't seen what had happened. So he picked up the paper.

And just before he was about to slip it back into the Bible his heart folded in on itself. He could barely make out the faint outline of Keira's name on the front of the paper. Written in pencil.

By him.

He slipped the paper back into the Bible, his heart now thundering in his chest. He remembered writing that note. He'd wanted to give Keira a valentine but had been too embarrassed to go into Aspen Valley and pick out a mushy card. He figured pink paper would be good enough for a valentine note. He remembered telling her in the note that one day he wanted her to be more than his valentine. He wanted her to be his wife.

Why did she still have it?

Same reason you still have that jackknife?

"Can you hold on to this while I sew these leathers on?" Keira asked, angling her chin toward the saddle she was manhandling onto a table beside her sewing machine. "I can do it by myself but since you're here you may as well make yourself useful."

Her sardonic tone made him smile. This was the Keira he had fallen in love with. The one he had written the note to.

"Your wish is my command," he said, thankful to have something to do while he sorted out his thoughts.

"Since when?" she challenged with a faint snort that was offset by her grin.

He held her gaze, a smile tugging at his lips. "You had more control over me than you realize."

"Past tense?"

She didn't miss a thing.

"The past was tense, but I have hopes for the future."

"Winning the NFR will make your future rosier?" she asked, raising her voice slightly above the thunk-thunk of the industrial sewing machine working its way through the many layers of worn leather.

"It will help."

Keira finished off the seam and cut the waxed thread, leaving long tails top and bottom for her to tie off later. She turned the saddle around and Tanner handed her the other leathers.

"Tell me again why it's so important to win this NFR for Roger?" she asked. Her tone was casual, but he saw a tension around her mouth and eyes.

Considering what she had told him last night, he wasn't sure what to say.

He pulled up a stool to get closer to her, hoping she would understand.

"You know how Roger died, didn't you?"

"I only heard it was an accident with a truck."

Tanner threaded his fingers together, the old guilt still so quick to haunt him. "I was supposed to drive him back to the hotel that night." He stopped a moment, trying to put the situation in perspective but still struggling to find an emotional distance. So quickly those agonizing "what-ifs" tormented him and pulled him back to that horrible night when he got the news. "But I didn't, and he died. I carry the burden of that. It was my fault. And I feel like the only way I can get rid of that is to finish what Roger had started."

"How do you think his death was your fault?"

Tanner paused, going back, yet again, to that night he wished he could relive. Redo.

"We had been at a rodeo after-party," he said, sinking back into a past where he spent far too much time. "Roger had just had a big win and was excited. I got tangled up in the saddle in my last competition and got hurt. I wanted to go back to the hotel and sleep. Things had been tense between us that day. Despite his win, Roger had been acting strange. Distant. Like he was ticked at me for something." Tanner paused, sighing as his thoughts slipped back to that tragic night, forever etched in his memory. "Fights seem to be a common theme between me and the people I care about," he said. "Anyway, Roger got all snarly and when I asked him what was wrong, he told me that he found out about the lawyer I hired to contest my dad's will. I don't know how he knew. I had just been feeling out my options. Alice had made it pretty clear Roger was getting the ranch if something happened to her. I felt marginalized. Pushed aside. I needed to know my rights."

"Must have been hard for Roger to know that if you got anything from the settlement, Roger would lose something," she said quietly. "He didn't like losing. Ever."

"You knew Roger as well as I did."

"But the ranch was your father's. You should have inherited half of it. Roger should not have been promised it all."

He easily heard the bitter note in her voice and, for a moment, wondered if something else had happened between her and Roger. He didn't want to think that his stepbrother, who not only stood to inherit his father's ranch, had also staked some claim on Keira's heart.

He pushed the treacherous thoughts aside and continued.

"I thought so, but I was only his stepchild. Or so Roger reminded me. I got angry, we fought and he said he was staying behind to party instead of coming to the hotel with me. He wanted to take some girl out and asked for my truck. I said no. Told him he'd been drinking. He got mad, one thing led to another and then he yelled at me. Told me that I wasn't his real brother. That a real brother wouldn't try to take his ranch away, which I suspect had been eating at him for a while. That I wasn't even our father's natural child. Well, that made me angrier. I gave him some money for a cab and left. On my way out I stopped a friend of ours and asked if he could make sure Roger got to the hotel on time."

Once again Tanner relived that moment just before he left Roger, that tug of hesitation, of wondering if Roger would listen to his warnings. "I shouldn't have left him. I should have stayed and driven him back to the hotel myself."

Keira stopped sewing and turned toward him, listening, Roger's saddle forgotten.

"Roger stayed at the party too long," Tanner continued, his attention focused on his thumbs tapping together. "Of course, he drank too much and used the cab money I gave him to buy more drinks. He couldn't find anyone to drive him back. Roger started walking back to the hotel. He was so drunk he wandered out into the street and was hit by a truck. He was killed instantly." Tanner stopped there, too easily remembering that early-morning phone call that had destroyed Tanner's world.

And dropped a burden on his shoulders he couldn't budge.

To his surprise he felt Keira put her hand on his arm. "It wasn't your fault," Keira said, echoing the words that everyone from his rodeo buddies to Monty and Ellen had tried to reassure him with.

The only one who didn't say them was Alice. Her silence clearly told him that she did, indeed, blame him for Roger's death. Her reproach was wordless but potent, and it only served to stoke the remorse haunting Tanner from that day on.

"Trouble was, he tried to call me. But I was in bed and my phone was in my jacket. I didn't hear it."

"Again, not your fault." Keira's hand tightened fractionally. "Roger always made his own choices. Always went his own way." The sharp tone in her voice caught his attention.

"I should have stayed, though," he said, dragging his gaze up to hers. "I should have made sure he got home okay. I should have kept my phone by the bed."

"You did what you could. You gave him cab money. You made sure someone was watching him. Knowing Roger, he was probably drunk, especially if he spent the money you gave him, as well. All of those were his decisions. His choices. None of them had anything to do with you." Her voice rose with each sentence, her anger, somehow, giving him some small comfort. It was the same anger he had dealt with over and over with no resolution. Except to finish this season for Roger.

He released a humorless laugh. "Yeah. I try to tell myself the same thing."

"So why don't you listen? You've always been a levelheaded guy. You're not a selfish, self-centered person. You've always cared about Roger. Everyone knows that."

Somehow Keira's praise was like a balm to a wound that had chafed for years. Keira, of all people, knew Roger as well as he had. Had grown up with him.

Had dated him.

He pushed that thought aside. That was in the past.

As was Roger's accident.

"Thanks," he said, looking up at her, holding her intent gaze.

"I mean it," she said, her voice quiet but fervent. "You're a good man. I've always thought that."

"Even after we broke up?"

She pressed her lips together, as if experiencing the pain of that again.

"I think we could have figured things out," he said quietly. "I know I should have told you about Dad's will. I was just angry about the ranch, and even though we were fighting, we had a good thing going. I know we did. I tried to make it up to you. I wanted us to get together again."

She slid her hand down and grabbed Tanner's hands, holding them between hers, squeezing them tightly as she shook her head.

"I know you did and...I'm sorry." She bit her lip, then looked into his eyes, her own glistening. "I'm sorry I didn't stay. I'm sorry..." Her voice broke off then.

Tanner could only stare at her, the import of what she was saying taking root. The sincerity in her voice igniting a spark of hope. He squeezed her hands back, a thrill coursing through him at the contact. It had been so long since he'd touched her. Since he'd been close to her.

And yet, he felt as if Roger still stood between them. After all, he had been the last person to see her before she left Aspen Valley.

"You didn't love him, did you?" The words burst out of him. He had to know. "Roger. You didn't love him?"

Keira slowly shook her head, her eyes locked on their intertwined hands. "Never. I just dated him because he wouldn't stop asking me. And...because he was your brother."

"What do you mean, because he was my brother?"

Another pause, as if she was holding something back. Then her finger made a delicate circle on his. A small opening.

"I guess, I hoped he would tell me something about you. Tell me what was happening in your life. It was a way of connecting with you, even if it was secondhand. I didn't hear anything from anyone about you. My parents didn't know, and I wasn't about to ask your stepmother." She finally looked up and gave him a rueful smile. "I didn't like her much right about then. But I knew you and Roger stayed in touch. I thought...he could tell me what was happening with you."

"Why did you need to know about me?" The question sounded like something a kid in high school would say. A deliberate question that he guessed the answer to already.

She didn't reply, but in her eyes he saw regret tinged with sorrow. "I didn't want us to be apart," she said quietly. "In spite of what happened. Despite me breaking up with you and then leaving Aspen Valley, I still wanted to be with you."

Questions remained about her hasty departure but somehow, sitting here with her, their hands intertwined, they were brushed aside as unnecessary. After many years of silence, they were together now. They were talking. And they were alone.

His sigh came from deep within his soul. "I missed you," he said, dropping his pride, thinking back to the note she still had tucked in her Bible.

"I missed you, too." She spoke so quietly he wasn't sure if she had spoken or if his own wishful thinking had created her words.

Then she blinked and it was the sparkle of tears in her eyes, the glistening track that an escaping tear made on her cheek that unmanned him. He could handle her anger, her aloofness, but her tears always broke down his defenses.

He gently brushed it away, his hand cupping her face, his thumb gently stroking her cheek. Her hand came up and she wrapped her fingers around his wrist.

Then, slowly, as if to give her an opportunity to stop him, Tanner bent closer and so carefully, as if dealing with a skittish horse, he brushed his lips over hers.

She pulled suddenly back, and he worried he had moved too quickly.

Then she lifted her hand and touched her lips. Her fingers trembled as she held his gaze. She looked up at him and once again he caught the hint of sorrow blended with fear.

"Can I kiss you again?" For some reason he felt he had to ask. The years apart, the silence; all combined to make him realize he couldn't assume they would immediately take up where they had left off.

"Maybe not yet?"

The *not* was a disappointment but the *yet* gave him hope.

But then she covered his hand with hers, a small sign of acceptance.

For now, that was enough.

BITS OF SUN struggled to peek through the gray, ragged clouds scudding across the sky. The storm had eased for now, but according to the forecast, they were due for another pounding of snow tonight. No one was getting to the ranch, and no one was leaving.

Keira stood just outside the shop, the chill of the air still making itself known, but it didn't matter.

Tanner's kiss still warmed her lips. It was a gentle, careful kiss, but it had rocked her to her core. As she had in the shop, she lifted her gloved fingers to her lips, as if testing the reality of that connection.

She closed her eyes, wondering if she dared to hope that this could work. That they could start over.

Dear Lord, she prayed, I'm scared. I hardly dare believe this could happen. Help me to trust that You'll take care of us.

Her thoughts slipped back to the Bible passage she had read this morning.

Forget the former things; do not dwell on the past. See, I am doing a new thing!

A new thing.

Keira drew in a cleansing breath of cold air and then slowly released it. Then once more. Each exhale released some tension, each inhale refreshed her.

A new thing. She had to stop dwelling on the past, and her reaction to Tanner's kiss gave her hope that they could start over.

At that, her thoughts moved to Alice. And for the first time since Roger's death, she wondered what Alice would do with the ranch. Would she ask Tanner to take over?

Would Tanner leave his shop in Lethbridge and come back to the ranch if Alice did ask?

She pushed those tentative notions aside, pulling herself back to the present. *Be in the moment,* she reminded herself. *Be content right here, right now.*

"Hey, you. Cows aren't going to get fed just standing around."

Tanner's deep voice behind her sent her heart fluttering, and as she turned around, his crooked smile and gentle eyes made it speed up even more.

They had just finished up their work on the saddle and now were heading out to feed the cows before going in for lunch.

"Hey, yourself," she returned, giving him a smile that sprang up from deep in her soul.

He took a step closer, dropped his arm over her shoulders just like he used to and gave her a quick, one-armed hug. She tensed a moment at the close contact. She caught the fleeting reaction in his eyes and then made herself relax. The past was gone. She and Tanner were moving on.

"You want me to drive?" he asked.

"Sure. The steering gets tight in this weather. It's not windy right now so I can walk behind you."

"You're coming in the cab with me again," Tanner said, not letting go of her shoulders as they plowed through the snow toward the machine shed. He gave her another squeeze and this time it was easier to lean into him. To fall into the familiar patterns of their past relationship.

He wore a heavy winter coat, and she had her parka on, but despite the layers between them, she felt the old connection slowly return.

"Besides, you can sit on my lap," he joked. "Like you used to."

"I was smaller then," she returned.

Tanner looked down at her then, his smile fading away. "I dunno. You look like you've lost weight to me."

"Don't you know that saying something like that is exactly the way to a girl's heart?"

"That and noticing a haircut," he returned, brushing her hair back from her face with a gloved hand.

She laughed, surprised at how quickly they fell into the old rhythms. And yet, as she looked up into his face, she saw lines that hadn't been there six years ago. The stubble that he seemed to favor now, shading his lean jaw, giving him an edgier look.

This was an older Tanner, and for an aching moment Keira felt the loss of the past six years.

She shook off the feeling as she pulled on the chain to open the overhead door while he climbed in the cab of the tractor and started it up. He let it run a moment and when he backed out, she lowered it again, the chain clanking loudly.

Tanner stopped the tractor just out the door of the shop, leaned over and opened the cab door. She clambered up into the

91

tractor, turned at an awkward angle to close the door behind her.

And then he pulled her onto his lap as he had promised.

"There's not much room here," she joked, wedged between him and the steering wheel. She tried to get up, but he grabbed on to her with one arm while he moved the seat back.

"There we go," he grunted, shifting his weight on the seat, still hanging on to her. "Comfy as all get out."

"No. Not really." She pushed away from him and, thankfully, this time he let her. Things were moving too quickly. She needed some time to adjust to this new relationship.

But as she managed to get off his lap in the lurching tractor, she steadied herself on his shoulder. Then kept her hand there. She caught the question in his eyes but stayed where she was. They hadn't seen each other for six years. That time apart couldn't be so quickly erased with just one kiss.

She hoped he understood.

But at the same time, a part of her wished she could sit on his lap like she used to. Act as if the breakup and all that had happened after that could simply be forgotten.

One step at a time, she reminded herself, realizing that for the first time in those lonely years, she felt as if she had something to look forward to.

She gave in to an impulse, lowered her head and brushed a quick kiss over his stubbled cheek. She caught his surprised expression in the mirror and then another one of his slow-release smiles that never failed to elicit a curl of awareness.

"Why you saucy little minx," Tanner teased, affecting an English accent the way he used to whenever he was feeling especially happy. "Distracting me while I'm driving. We could end up in a snowbank."

She grinned, thankful for his acceptance of her actions. "If that's all it takes—"

What she said was cut off by his sudden swinging of the tractor toward the snow.

"Don't get stuck," she squealed, clinging to him while the tractor rode up the snowbank, tilting to one side. "We'll never be able to pull this thing out."

"I won't get stuck," he said, manhandling it back onto the track. "I always know my limits."

"Like the time you ended up swimming that river, clinging to Hardisty's saddle because you didn't think the spring runoff was that strong," she teased, her hand clinging tightly to his shoulder now.

"I got me and that horse across, didn't I?" he challenged her, his dark eyes sparkling at her in the mirror of the tractor.

"About a mile farther downstream than you were supposed to."

"Mile is better than a miss," he misquoted.

Keira caught his answering grin.

"We had some good times, didn't we?"

His voice held more than a question. It was as if he was seeking verification of the years they spent together.

"We had a lot of good times," she said with conviction. "The best years of my life so far were the ones I spent with you."

She caught the curiosity in his eyes. As if he was wondering, if her statement was true, what had she been doing with Roger. Why they had stayed apart.

Her only answer was a careful smile, which he returned. It softened his features, and she felt the all-too-familiar flip of her heart. Old emotions rose, old feelings that pushed at the events of the past six years.

They made quick work of feeding the cows as the sun struggled to streak through the breaking clouds. Tanner scraped some of the snowdrifts away from the feeders and made a path around them to make it easier for the cattle to eat. An hour later the tractor was parked back in the shop, and they were headed back to the house.

"You can't even see that I shoveled these walks yesterday," he complained as they slogged through the drifts that had gathered overnight. "Thank goodness the snow quit for now. Though we're supposed to get more tonight."

"Dad said the plows were just starting to open up the main highways."

"Does he know if he'll make it back to the ranch in time for your mom's dinner?"

Keira wondered at his question. Wondered if he was anxious to go.

"He's not sure. Even if the highways are plowed, it'll be a while before our roads are done. We're not on a school bus route so we're not a priority."

They entered the porch the same time Alice did, Adana's piercing cries accompanying her. The toddler was crying, waving her arms, leaning away from Alice, her mouth open, her eyes full of tears.

"What's wrong?" Keira asked, tugging her knitted hat off her head and pulling off her mittens.

"She won't settle down. I think she wants to go outside. I know John takes her out for a walk every day. She must be feeling cooped up."

Keira looked at the little girl, who was reaching out to her, her blue eyes brimming with tears, her blond curls in disarray.

"Oh, muffin," Keira murmured, taking the girl in her arms. "You getting cabin fever?"

Adana stared at Keira then leaned toward the door. "'Side," she said in a plaintive tone. "Go 'side."

"I thought I could take her out." Alice gathered Adana's clothes off one of the hooks in the porch.

"What about Ellen?" Tanner asked.

Alice didn't say anything, but Keira could tell that she was uncomfortable leaving her mother behind.

"I can take her out," Keira said. "I'm already dressed."

Alice's look of relief made Keira feel kindlier to the woman. "That would be wonderful. I'm sure she'll have more fun with you than with me." Alice was about to hand Keira the girl's coat and snow pants when Tanner took them from her.

"Sit down on the box," he said. "I'll help you get her dressed."

"Do you know how?" Keira teased as she turned Adana around in her arms. The girl had settled somewhat, as if she knew something was happening.

Tanner held up the snow pants as Keira sat down on the box. "These first." Then he held up the mittens. "Then the boots. The coat goes on next and this hat thingy last."

"Wow, you must have taken classes or something."

"Or something," he said with a grin. "Or maybe I just know in which order I put on my own winter clothes."

"Makes sense," Keira said as Tanner slipped the pants on the wriggling little girl. Keira set her down so they could work the straps over her shoulders.

"'Side. 'Side," Adana called out, reaching her hands toward the door.

"How does John do this?" Keira asked as she attempted to tug mittens on Adana's hands.

"This would go faster if you would cooperate, sweetie," Tanner muttered as he grabbed one of her wiggling feet, struggling to get the boot on.

Keira couldn't keep her eyes off Tanner as he patiently worked the boot on the little girl's foot. Adana wasn't cooperating but Tanner persisted.

When they finally got her dressed, Keira set Adana on the porch floor so she could put on her own mittens. The little girl, hampered by the bulky clothing, promptly fell on her behind. Her look of surprise made Keira laugh out loud.

"I'm getting her out of here before she starts crying," Tanner said, scooping her up in one arm. He dropped his hat on his head and with Adana tucked up against him, headed out the door.

Keira was right behind him. "I think there's a sled in the woodshed," she said, veering off through the snowdrifts they hadn't had a chance to clear away yet.

She found it and pulled it along behind her as she waded through the deep snow, the plastic shell bumping along behind her.

Tanner had set Adana in a snowbank while he shoveled what snow he could away from the door of the house. The little girl was quiet but as soon as she saw the sled she waved her arms, her cries of excitement echoing in the chill winter air.

"Okay, Adana, I get the hint," Tanner said. He set the shovel aside and picked her up. He handed Keira the girl as he took the sled away from Keira. "Climb on with her."

"I'm too heavy."

Tanner just raised his eyebrows at her.

"No. Seriously. You'll never be able to pull me around."

Tanner tapped her nose with his gloved finger. "Stop arguing with me, Latigo Kid, and just get on the sled already. Adana will fall over otherwise. Besides, I'm not going to pull you around all by myself. We're going to use the snow machine."

"Are you sure?"

"I won't go fast." He gave her a wide grin. "Trust me."

She held his eyes a moment, then smiled. In this, she could trust him.

And with the other stuff?

She subdued the thought and settled on the sled. *One day at a time,* she reminded herself. *One day at a time.*

CHAPTER EIGHT

"*H*old on to Adana," Tanner called out to Keira above the whine of the snow machine's engine. "I'm going for broke."

A long rope at the back of the machine was tied to the sled, and as he squeezed the throttle and the machine sped up across the open field, he heard Keira's squeal. He looked behind him, through the spray of snow kicked up by the machine, and the sight of Keira's laughing grin and Adana's excitement made him laugh, as well. But he wasn't looking ahead, and the sled went off the trail he had made, veering sideways. Tanner immediately slowed down but it was too late. The sled wobbled then tipped, dumping Keira and Adana into the soft, fluffy snow.

Tanner hit the brakes and jumped off the machine, immediately ending up in snow almost to his thighs. By the time he got to the upturned sled, Keira was already on her feet, brushing snow off Adana, who, to Tanner's surprise, was screeching with delight.

All Tanner could see of the bundled-up little girl were her eyes, wide with anticipation.

"Again," she called out, her voice muffled by the snow-encrusted scarf. "Again!"

"Obviously she's okay," Tanner said as he brushed snow off Keira's coat. "Are you?"

Snow clung to her eyelashes, stocking cap, and mittens. But her eyes sparkled with a happiness he hadn't seen since he came to the ranch.

"I'm fine," she said as she set Adana on the now righted sled. "But I don't think it's fair that we got all covered with snow and you didn't."

And before Tanner could guess at what she was going to do, she gave him a quick shove. He tried to catch his balance, but he fell backward into the snow, looking up at the sky, silvery flakes fluttering down and melting on his face. Keira was laughing.

"That's real funny," he said, struggling to his feet, shivering as some snow melted and slithered down the back of his neck. "Hilarious."

She must have seen the intent in his eyes. Squealing, she turned to grab Adana for protection, but Tanner hooked his arm around her waist before Keira could pick up the little girl. He swung her around, but Keira wasn't going down without a fight. She grabbed him as he was about to toss her and they fell into the snow together, snow flying up around them.

Behind them Adana laughed her appreciation of their stunts.

"Well, I guess we're even." Keira laughed, trying to release herself from Tanner's arms.

But they had gone too far off the track and were swamped in the deep snow. Tanner couldn't get any purchase in the loose snow and Keira, lying beside him, couldn't move.

They struggled, but each movement drew them deeper into the snow, like quicksand.

Still laughing, Tanner stopped his struggles, trying to figure out how to get out of there.

He blinked the snow out of his eyes and looked down at

Keira, still trapped under him, his one arm buried in the snow beside her head, his other hand resting on her shoulder. She was grinning, two lumps of snow decorating her cheeks.

They lay still for a moment, the silence of the day falling like a blanket on them. Their eyes held. Tanner couldn't look away. Her smile wavered and then her expression grew serious.

Slowly, giving her the opportunity to stop him, he lowered his head. She didn't move. Didn't stop him. He brought his cold lips to hers.

She lay utterly still, then moved toward him, holding the kiss. Keira's arm came around his neck, pulling him closer. And the spark of hope that had been kindled by their shared kiss this morning grew to a steady glow.

The differences, the years apart, the arguments all faded away in this mutual kiss.

Adana's burbling slowly eased into the moment and, reluctantly, Tanner pulled away.

"Guess we should get up," Keira said, her voice breathless. But she didn't move right away.

Tanner shot a look over his shoulder, but Adana still sat on the sled, happily batting at some snow stuck to her mitten.

He shifted and finally managed to find solid ground. Or solid enough to stand up. Keira was sitting up now, and he grabbed her hand, pulling her to her feet. She wobbled, then caught him by the arm.

Again, their eyes met. Again, Tanner felt as if the world had narrowed down to just the two of them. He didn't want reality to intrude. He wanted to hang on to this moment forever.

But Adana needed them, and the snow that had been so magical just a few moments ago was slowly melting down the back of his neck.

"We should get going," Keira said, her voice breathless.

Tanner kept his hold on her arm as they stumbled about in the deep snow, working their way to the track of the snow machine. Finally, they could walk easier, and Keira went directly to the sled, crouching down in front of Adana.

"You okay, monkey? Sorry for abandoning you like that."

Tanner couldn't keep his eyes off Keira with the little girl. Nor could he stop the nudge of melancholy at the sight. If his father hadn't willed the ranch entirely to Alice when he died, if Tanner hadn't had to go work in Lethbridge and take on as many rodeos as he could…maybe they would have been married and had their own child by now.

The weight of all those "ifs" dropped like a stone on his heart as he realized how many things needed to be exactly right to maintain their relationship.

Sorrow and regret spiraled through him. Did they ever have a chance?

Maybe not then, but what about now?

The question taunted him. What had changed to make what was starting again between them possible?

He and Keira were older and wiser now, and not as foolishly optimistic. If things were beginning between them again, they would be entering this relationship with their eyes wide open.

But even as these thoughts were formulated, he knew she would have to answer questions about the six-year silence somewhere along the way.

He just hoped he would be happy with the answers.

Make eye contact. Keep your cool. Don't back down like you always did.

Keira stared Tanner down, trying to take his measure.

He held her gaze, his eyes narrowed.

"What are you up to? What are you scheming?"

"Just watch."

She couldn't keep the triumph out of her voice as she looked down then carefully laid out the wooden tiles on the Scrabble board, pluralizing the one Tanner had just laid out as well as landing on a double word score.

Adana was down for the night. Supper was over and the four adults were spending the evening together.

"That's thirty-eight points," she said triumphantly, totaling her score and scribbling it on the notepad. "Beat that, Tanner Fortier."

"Wait a minute. *Bators* isn't a word." Tanner leaned forward in his chair, squinting at the letters Keira had just placed on the board.

"It is the pluralized form of people who hunt alligators using live fish. Bators." Keira reached for the small velvet bag that held the rest of the letters she needed, trying to look confident and casual.

"I've never heard of that one," her mother said, looking up from the scarf she was painstakingly knitting. Keira couldn't understand why her mother had taken over the project from her. The neck brace made looking down awkward and it had taken Ellen hours to get even the little bit done she had. But she was smiling so it mustn't have bothered her too much.

"It's not that well-known," Keira returned.

"Don't you have a dictionary?" Alice looked up from the photo album on her lap she was paging through. "You could look it up in there, Tanner."

"We had a Scrabble dictionary, but it was lost years ago." In fact, Tanner had hidden it one time when he and Keira were having a lively game of Scrabble the last time they had played, and he was the one making up words.

And there it was again. That familiar ache at the thought of that more innocent time. Times when Tanner spent most every evening here to get away from the constant sniping between Alice and Cyrus.

"It would be in the dictionary," Keira said, setting her new tiles on her slate. "Under the *B*'s."

"You're really going with that?" Tanner challenged her. "I could do a search on my phone if I had it handy."

"And if you would, you would find out that I'm right." Keira held his gaze, trying not to grin.

"Okay. I see we're playing with *those* rules." He pursed his lips in concentration as he rearranged the tiles on his slate and Keira could see from the sudden gleam in his eye that he had an idea. He turned the board around on the turntable Keira's father had made especially for playing Scrabble, then quickly laid out his tiles.

Keira tried to read his word upside down, but she couldn't make it out.

"So that empties my slate, pluralizes goose and I get a triple word score, which gives me a total of…" He added up the numbers using his fingers like he always did. "A whopping one hundred and twenty-three points." He angled his chin toward the score pad. "Write that down, Latigo Kid."

Keira turned the board and smothered a laugh when she read his word. "*Imsyncts?* What in the world does that mean?"

"It's a group of young girls who do karaoke to boy band music."

"I don't believe you. Besides, the word goose pluralizes is geese."

"Not in my world."

Keira chuckled. "I'll have to give you fifty extra points just for creativity."

"Don't need them," Tanner said as he filled up his slate. "I'm taking you down without those pity points."

As her laughter pealed out, their eyes met again. His gaze softened and his hand slid across the table and caught hers. As their fingers twined together Keira felt her life shifting into a familiar, wonderful place.

Could this happen? she wondered. Could they truly start over?

"Oh, my goodness, Tanner, look at these pictures," Alice said, getting up from her chair, her attention on the photo album she was carrying. She set it down on the table beside them, her finger resting on a photo at the top of the page.

Had she done that on purpose? Had she seen Tanner take her hand? Her sudden interruption seemed rather timely.

Tanner withdrew his hand and dutifully looked at the album.

The picture was of the three of them. Roger, Tanner, and Keira, all on horseback.

"Look how young you all were," Alice said, a note of sorrow in her voice. "I don't think Roger was much more than eight in this photo. Is that Hardisty he's riding?"

Tanner shook his head. "No. Hardisty was just a colt then. I think that's Babe."

"Oh, that's right. Roger raised her from a colt and trained her, as well." Alice released a light sigh. "Didn't Heather ride her once in one of her barrel racing competitions?"

"She did. I think she won," Tanner said, gamely playing along.

Keira remembered the story differently, however. Tanner was the one who spent the most time training Babe and had done most of the difficult groundwork. By the time Roger took over, Babe was broke to ride with a saddle. He just did some of the finishing touches, such as neck reining and teaching her to change leads and back up and ground tie.

"Roger had as much of a way with animals as he did with people."

"That's not saying much." As soon as the words spilled out, Keira wished she could pull them back, bury them where they belonged. Especially when she caught Alice's frown.

"Roger was a kind young man with many friends," Alice replied with an injured tone. "

Keira forced a smile, wondering if she could try to pass her comment off as a joke to ease the tension. But she was tired of hearing how wonderful Roger was when, in fact, he was anything but.

"He had lots of friends, but he was no angel," Keira said quietly.

Alice picked up the photo album and straightened, holding it against her as if using it for protection. "I realize that, but he was a good boy. And he was my son."

"I'm sorry," Keira murmured.

Her apology was automatic, and it felt like dust in her mouth. Her heart twisted in her chest, and she suddenly felt claustrophobic.

"If you'll excuse me," she muttered. "I forgot I have to get some work done in the office."

She ignored Tanner's frown and Alice's pinched look as she got up from the table, restraining herself from rushing through the living room to the sanctuary of her father's office. She didn't have anything to do there, but she needed to get away from Alice.

The room was dark and empty and as she dropped into the chair behind the desk, she felt the weight of the past few years drop onto her shoulders, as well. She turned the chair to look out the window but all she saw was her vague reflection in the darkened glass and the glow from the doorway. She had forgotten to close the door and could hear the murmur of conversation from the living room.

She knew her sudden departure would generate a flood of questions, but she was getting tired of how Alice constantly brought Roger into every moment she spent with Tanner. It was as if she was reminding Keira of her brief relationship with Roger.

Would Roger always be there? Would he always be hovering

in the background, a shadowy reminder of the years she and Tanner had lost?

She thought all of that would have died with Roger, but apparently not.

She shivered a moment; suddenly bone-weary, sadness washed over her as she pulled her legs up against her chest. She and Tanner had lost so much.

"You okay?" Tanner spoke quietly from the doorway, but it still made her heart jump.

She looked up and saw Tanner's shadowy reflection in the window.

"Yeah. I'm fine," she said, turning around, hoping she sounded more offhand than she felt.

Tanner walked into the darkened office, his hands shoved in the front pockets of his pants, shoulders hunched like he always did when he wasn't sure of her mood, his features shadowed except for the glint of his eyes.

"You don't seem fine. Was it what my mother said about Roger that bothered you?"

Confused sorrow coiled through her and Keira knew she couldn't get away with evading the topic. "I just wish your stepmother would leave Roger dead and buried," she finally said.

"What do you mean?"

"We were having such a fun time, you and me, just like we used to, and she has to ruin things with her photo album and her stories and her distorted view of Roger." She stopped, hearing the rising anger in her voice.

Tanner came around the desk, caught her hands and, as she lowered her feet to the floor, gently pulled her upright. Then he turned, sat in the chair himself and pulled her onto his lap.

"Your hands are freezing," he said, slipping his arms around her.

Keira leaned into his embrace, allowing herself this moment

of support and strength. *It had been so long,* she thought, laying her head on Tanner's shoulder.

"I think it bothers Alice to see us together," Tanner said finally. "Maybe she thought you deserved someone like Roger more than someone like me."

Keira caught Tanner's face between the palms of her hands. "Don't even let that sinister thought land in your brain," she said, tightening her hands to emphasize her point. "Ever."

"To tell you the truth, it may have landed but it didn't take root." He gave her a smile, his teeth a flash of white in the soft darkness of the office, his eyes shining in the light coming from the door. He stroked her hair back from her face and his smile slipped away. "Trouble was, I never felt like I deserved you, either."

"It was the other way around," she said quietly.

Thankfully Tanner didn't ask her to elaborate and instead he moved his hand to her back, making gentle circles with the palm of his hand. Just like he used to.

Keira allowed herself this moment of just being close to him with no one else around. Finally, she curled her hand behind Tanner's neck and lowered her head to his shoulder, easing out a contented sigh. "I don't want to talk about Alice. Or Roger," she said as she closed her eyes, treasuring this moment as his arms tightened around her. "I just want to be us. You and me. Right now."

"I like that idea," Tanner said, resting his cheek on her head. His chest lifted as he drew in a long, deep breath. "I missed this. I missed us."

His last three words dove into her soul and for a moment she had to fight tears back. "I missed us, too."

She felt Tanner tense ever so slightly, as if he wanted to ask something more, but then, thankfully, he simply leaned back, rocking her gently. They sat in the dark silence, letting the moment lengthen.

Then Tanner drew his head back and cupped her face. He smiled down at her and then, once again, kissed her, his mouth moving slowly over her lips, igniting a glow of pleasure, of yearning.

Keira leaned into the kiss, her hands clinging to his neck, her lips shifting, tasting, exploring.

After some time, they pulled away, each breathless.

Keira laid her head back on his shoulder, tucking it against his neck, treasuring this moment of connection.

"Did I ever tell you how beautiful you are?" he asked.

"Not for a while."

He grew serious. "Lot of water under the bridge," he said quietly. "One of these days we'll catch up."

His words held a promise of a future but at the same time she felt a shiver of premonition. One of these days she'd have to tell him everything.

But would he believe her?

CHAPTER NINE

"*L*ooks like we'll be home Saturday at the earliest," Monty was saying over the cell phone.

The connection wasn't the best, so his voice crackled and broke a couple of times, but Tanner eventually caught the gist of the conversation.

He stood in the lee of the leather-working shop, leaning against the wall, out of the wind. This morning sun was shining, and the temperature had risen, but the fields ahead of him were still one long unbroken expanse of snow, whipped up by the wind that still blew. "That's great. Are the roads clearing up where you are?"

"They're mostly clear here and I guess it's all clear to Aspen Valley. Have the plow trucks been to the ranch yet?"

"No. I cleared out the driveway this morning, but the road is still snowed in."

Wednesday they thought they'd had a reprieve from the storm, but the winds started up again yesterday and more snow had come down last night. Ellen's birthday had been a bleak day and dinner had been a simple meal. Today, however, they had woken up to a clear blue sky and the promise of warmer weather.

"Well, let me know when they come," Monty said. "John and I will travel as far as we can, then hole up until we can go farther. I should call Ellen, and John wants to find out how Adana is."

"She's fine. Keira and I took her out to play in the snow the other day..."

"She must have enjoyed that. I know John always complains that he doesn't spend enough time with her."

"It was fun." That three-letter word was too small to describe what had happened that afternoon. It had been so much more than fun. It was a glimpse of possibilities.

"I can't tell you enough how much I appreciate you sticking around there to help out. I think God knew I needed you there."

Tanner suspected God knew a whole lot more than that. "I'm glad I could be here," he said, his lame response hardly able to encompass the myriad of emotions he had dealt with the past few days and was still dealing with.

"Well, I better get going," Monty said. "Got a few miles to go and John's antsy to see Adana. We both feel bad that we missed Ellen's birthday."

"Ellen just wants you home safe. She said we can celebrate next week instead."

"That'd be great." Monty said goodbye and ended the call.

Tanner dropped his phone into his coat pocket and pulled his gloves on. The sun was out in full force today. Last night and this morning, wind from the storm had piled a few more drifts on the yard but it had also scrubbed the sky clear of clouds and brought in some warmer temperatures.

When the wind quit it was going to be a beautiful day in many ways.

When Monty had called, he and Keira had just finished

checking the cows. Then Keira had gone ahead of him to the shop to finish up her work on Roger's saddle.

Tanner waited a moment before going into the shop, his mind ticking back to last night. After their simple dinner he and Keira had again gone to Monty's office to spend some time alone. They had chatted about inconsequential things. She'd told him a few stories about people in and around Aspen Valley and got him caught up on the local gossip.

He'd shared some stories from the road. She'd told him about the years she spent in Edmonton, away from the ranch. Slowly it seemed the time between was getting filled in. They'd talked about things they were thankful for, one of which was being together again.

Their 'chats' were interspersed with kisses that grew longer and more urgent. He knew they had to be careful, but he felt as if they had years of connecting to catch up on.

However, always hanging over his head was Alice and the status of his father's ranch. He knew Aspen Valley and the ranch were home to Keira. He tried to picture her in Lethbridge, living in either a cramped apartment or a small house on a lot not much bigger than the space the ranch house took up. He could give her a comfortable life, Lethbridge wasn't a huge city, and the open range wasn't far out of town, but he couldn't give her what she had here at Refuge Ranch.

Should he talk to the lawyer again? Should he push the situation? Was it too late?

His father's willing of the ranch to Alice without any provision for him had deep consequences for his life and the fact that he couldn't even confront the man who had done it had resonated through the past six years.

After Roger's death, he had to stop himself again and again from phoning Alice to ask her, what now? He knew that she was renting some of the land, but would he be able to lease it once that term was up? Tanner had money set aside and a business he could sell. He would even be willing to pay Alice for half of the ranch, though the thought galled. As did the amount of money he would have to come up with.

In the shop behind him, Keira was putting the final touches on Roger's saddle. His original plan was to be back in Lethbridge right now, checking in at the shop and then heading over to his friend's place close to Vegas, where he would spend the days before the NFR practicing. Getting himself into the right place mentally to do what he'd set out to do from the beginning of this tour.

Win the NFR for his stepbrother.

But somehow, the past few days had changed his sense of urgency. Diluted it. He had other priorities now that interfered with his big plans. His heart was torn between assuaging the guilt that hung like a shadow in his life and the changing relationship with the girl who had never left his thoughts.

Show me what I should do, Lord. Help me to have the right reasons for what I do. The right motives.

He pushed himself away from the shed. His prayer life hadn't been the most robust of late. His busy schedule didn't lend itself to maintaining a strong relationship with the Lord. But at the same time, he always knew his faith was like the roots of a tree that dug down into his very being. So much a part of him, he knew it would never leave.

Keira looked up from the saddle when he stepped into the shop and gave him a wide smile. "It's coming along," she said. "Another day's work should do it."

Tanner just nodded, unable to generate a lot of excitement about that fact.

Do you have to go?

The words taunted and tantalized.

"What did my dad want?" she asked, making the stirrup leathers damp in preparation for a design she was going to stamp on them.

"Just to let me know that they're on their way. The main roads are clear. We'll just have to wait for the plow trucks to come up our road to clear it out before they can come home."

Keira picked up a couple of stamps and held them up. "Which one do you prefer? The twisted rope or the barbed-wire pattern? The old one had a stamp pattern that we don't have anymore."

Tanner didn't really care. "The barbed-wire one is similar enough to the pattern on the cantle."

Keira nodded but her smile held an edge. "I'm glad that Dad and John will be able to come home soon," she said quietly, picking up her hammer. "When do you have to go back to Lethbridge?"

"I just called the guys. We didn't get the mechanic contract for that trucking company, so work is manageable right now. I guess I can stay for a few days yet, but I absolutely have to leave on Monday."

"Will you come back for our belated birthday party?"

He heard her expectant tone. The faint bubble of happiness. He tried not to think of what had to happen before he could get to the NFR. Ellen's birthday do-over was a few days away. He was supposed to have been at his garage the past two days, then at his friend's place, going over his strategy. Practicing. Getting back to his workout routine, something he'd been neglecting since coming here.

Everything he'd worked for was coming at him.

Then he caught Keira's smile and felt an age-old tremor in his heart.

And he knew that staying here with Keira was anything but a distraction. It was a situation rife with possibilities and potential.

"I think I can," he said, taking a step closer and pulling her into his arms, needing the reality of her presence to remind him what was the most important thing in his life. Yes, there were questions yet, but this was Keira. The only girl who had ever held his heart.

"I know I can," he amended. "I'll make it work."

He curbed the sense of panic at the change in his plans. Then she looked up at him, her smile wide and expectant. When he kissed her the panic shifted to hope.

It would all work out, he told himself as he rested his head on Keira's.

It had to.

KEIRA FLUFFED out the skirt of the brown-and-white polka-dotted dress she'd pulled out of her closet, giving herself a critical once-over in the full-length mirror in her bedroom. It had been years since she wore a dress to church, usually preferring to wear pants or capris. In fact, it had been years since she'd worn a dress, period.

She suppressed a shiver, then a couple of figures in the yard caught her attention. She walked to the window to get a closer look. Her father and Tanner were walking back from the corrals and even from here Keira could see the smile on her father's face. John and her father had come home yesterday as glad to be home as Ellen and Keira were to have them back.

Her father and Tanner stopped a moment, laughing, looking as natural together as her father always had with Lee.

Keira pressed her hand against her aching heart, thinking of her brother so far from home, her sister now divorced but still living in New York.

Please, Lord, she prayed, *watch over my brother and sister. Take care of Lee. Help him to get over his guilt. To let him know he is forgiven and can come home. Take care of Heather. Keep her safe.*

She tried not to worry about her sister. Heather was a smart girl, she reminded herself. She knew how to take care of herself.

She watched as her father and Tanner split up—Tanner to the bunkhouse on the ranch he'd moved back to after the storm and Monty to the house.

Then she glanced at the clock beside her bedside table and her thoughts shifted from the future to the present. Tanner said he would pick her up at nine-thirty for church. It was already nine-fifteen. She stepped across the hall to the bathroom to finish getting ready.

Alice was walking toward her, carrying an armful of towels that Keira presumed were for her mother. She started when she saw Keira, surprise etched on her features. "My goodness, you look lovely," she said.

Keira felt suddenly self-conscious and had to stop herself from brushing her hands over her dress. "Thought I would dress up today," she said.

"For church?"

"Yeah. I know Dad wants to stay home with Mom, but Tanner and I are going. He's coming to get me in a few moments."

"You and Tanner?"

Was it her imagination or did she hear the faintest note of censure in her voice?

"Well, you look lovely," Alice repeated. "I haven't seen you in a dress since…" Her voice drifted off, as if Alice was recalling the memory.

"It's been a while," Keira agreed and ducked into the bathroom, hoping to forestall any further conversation. She was already running late.

She closed the door behind her and leaned against it, unable to shrug off the feelings Alice created in her. One of these days she was going to have to make peace with Alice. One day.

She pushed herself away from the door, plugged in her curling iron and ducking down, pulled out a basket of makeup she also hadn't used in a long while. As she got ready, her hands trembled with nervous excitement.

It took her a few tries, and thankfully she didn't burn herself, but finally she got her hair the way she liked it, her makeup just fine. She hooked some gold hoops in her ears, gave herself another critical once-over and allowed herself a flutter of expectation.

She was just about ready when she heard her father calling up to her that Tanner was here. She caught her flushed cheeks and bright eyes in the mirror, gave herself a smile of encouragement, pulled a white blazer over her dress and ran down the stairs to meet him.

Tanner stood just inside the living room wearing a white shirt and blue jeans, his hat in his hands. The look of shocked surprise on his face was worth every second thought she'd had while she was getting ready.

A few minutes later she was sitting in Tanner's truck, sitting an appropriate distance away from him, the flutter growing. Tanner turned the key then shot her a lazy smile. "You look amazing," he said quietly.

Her cheeks warmed at his compliment as she looked down at her dress and high-heeled boots. "I know it's not the most practical outfit to wear, what with all the snow—"

"You're beautiful," he said, stopping her as he put the truck in Reverse and backed up.

Her cheeks grew even warmer as she gave him a shy smile. "Thanks. And I'm glad you decided to come to church. I wasn't looking forward to going on my own again."

"No problem. I could tell your dad just wanted to spend some time with your mom, and John just looked beat."

"I hope Adana lets him sleep in."

"Guy's got a lot on his plate. Losing his wife. Taking care of a little girl alone."

"He's a good man. I'd always hoped that he and Heather would make a go of it," she said with a heavy sigh.

"Heather wanted more out of life than living out on a ranch, I think," Tanner said as they drove down the road.

"I can't blame her. She's had so little before Mom and Dad adopted her."

Tanner just smiled. "You know what? Much as I love your family, I'd sooner talk about us."

"Us? There's an us?" She tossed out the question with a playful note, as if it didn't cost her everything to ask.

"I think we both know there's an us," he said quietly.

Keira didn't think her smile could get any wider. "So, what about us did you want to talk about?"

Tanner was quiet a moment, the hum of the truck tires on the snowy road the only sound in the cab of the truck. "So, when you left Aspen Valley, what did you do?"

Her heart raced but then she took a breath, quieting herself. His question was simply a way of catching up, filling in the gaps of their separate lives, Keira reminded herself. Just like he'd said they should.

"I moved to Edmonton and got a job there as a waitress," she said, looking ahead at the road, trying not to delve too far back. "Same work I did at the Grill and Chill when we were dating."

"Did you know someone there? Is that why you chose Edmonton?"

"No. I just wanted to be somewhere different than Aspen Valley."

"Did you like it there?"

She'd hated most every minute of it but admitting to that would only lead to questions that would take her places she didn't want to go. "I didn't mind it. I had a few adventures, made a few friends, but I was glad to return to the ranch and do what I always enjoyed. Helping my dad with the leatherwork."

"And now you've expanded," he said.

"Business is good. At one time I thought of setting up a shop in town, but my dad didn't want me to leave so for now, I'm happy working here."

"Any other plans for the business?" Tanner asked, turning the truck one-handed onto the highway.

"A few. I want to hire someone more permanently to help me with the piecework. I want to set up a website and do internet orders. I've had several requests for that whenever we do a trade show. I need more trade show equipment."

"Like what?"

"Some custom backgrounds. A few more display racks. A better table where I can do business. That kind of thing."

"Sounds ambitious."

"I like the work and I feel like I've brought it to a new level."

"No more saddle work?"

"I'd do some, but I'd have to hire someone to help me with that."

"Maybe you could teach me."

She shot him a look, wondering if he was teasing. And though his mouth was quirked up in his familiar half smile that usually denoted some form of mockery, she caught a glint in his eyes that softened it.

"Would you want to do that? Trade in your wrenches for a sewing machine?"

"Well, when you talk about it like that, I'm not so sure." He laughed, but then grew serious again. "I've always liked working in the shop with your dad. I knew a few things. I'm a fast learner. I think I could put a saddle together with the right teacher."

There it was again. That hint of a promise. A vague glimpse of a future.

"And what about you?" she asked. "What did you do after... after we broke up?"

Tanner shrugged and his mouth shifted into the partial smile that could either be construed as cynical or as teasing. "You know already. Worked. Rodeoed. Tried to outrun the shadows of Roger's death." He glanced sidelong at her and his smile shifted toward cynical.

Then he looked away and in the silence that drifted up between them, Keira knew Tanner's questions hadn't been answered.

Please, Lord, she prayed. Let me know what to do. What to say.

But not yet, she thought, catching his crooked smile as he reached across the cab for her hand. She put her hand in his, curling her fingers around his, letting his large, rough hand warm hers.

Not yet.

CHAPTER TEN

"Y ou're still around?" Quinn DeVries asked as he walked alongside Tanner out of church. "I thought you had to head out to Lethbridge."

Tanner looked up at his old friend and shrugged. Tanner was tall, but he always felt short around Quinn, who was easily six-four. With his dark hair and easygoing smile, Tanner was surprised Quinn hadn't been snapped up by any of the single girls in Aspen Valley.

"Yeah. Got a good reason to stay." Tanner glanced behind him at Keira, who had been detained by Brooke and Freya, who he caught looking at him with eagerness in their expressions. They looked immediately away, but it wasn't too hard to guess they were talking about him.

"I kind of guessed that. Keira's looking a lot happier than she has for a long time," Quinn said, adding a wink.

Tanner smiled at the comment, which also ignited a spark of hope. He still felt as if he and Keira were carefully finding their way around this new relationship, but he was starting to look past the next day. Starting to let the vague promise of a future settle in his mind.

"If you got some time, I need to talk to you," Quinn DeVries said as they made their way to the foyer of the church.

"You sound serious," Tanner said, shooting another glance back to see if Keira was coming. He hoped they could go out for lunch afterward. Spend some time alone, away from the ranch. He turned his attention back to Quinn. "I don't have a lot of time. I need to head back to Lethbridge tomorrow, spend a couple of days there to make sure I still have a shop and some employees." He had called the shop foreman last night and had received a favorable report. But he had also gotten a call from a dissatisfied customer, so he had to deal with that, as well. "But talk to me now, if you have the time. Keira will be a while."

Quinn caught his lip between his teeth, as if thinking, then angled his head to a quieter corner of the foyer. "Follow me," he said.

They walked through people tugging coats off hangers; mothers and fathers crouched down teasing mittens on reluctant hands, pulling stocking caps on turning heads.

"So, what do you need to tell me?" Tanner asked when they stopped.

"It's not a huge deal. I didn't want anyone to overhear, but I thought, now that you're back, I'd like to try get out of the lease I have on Alice's ranch."

Even after all this time, calling it Alice's ranch still created a roil of agitation. "Why would you want to do that?"

"I know I've got a year left, but Elyse Whitaker approached me about her land. She wants to set up a lease to own, but she wants us to start this spring. That would mean I'd have to back out of the lease on Alice's. Elyse's place is perfect. It's right beside mine. I could get my brother Lucas back to Aspen Valley and on board, but I can't afford to lease two ranches and run my own."

"So why do you need to talk to me about that?"

"Well, now that you're back, I thought you would be taking over the Circle C and running it."

"I don't know if I'm 'back' per se," Tanner said, but even as he edged around Quinn's comment, he knew that he was closer and closer to finding a way to make that happen. "I'm just taking things one day at a time for now," Tanner conceded. "But I'll talk to Alice about the lease. I'm back Wednesday night for Ellen's birthday dinner at Refuge Ranch. I can let you know then."

"That's soon enough." Quinn eased out a smile, then started walking toward the foyer. "And I'm looking forward to seeing you at the NFR."

"I hope so. Got a lot riding on it."

"Proud of you, friend. You'll do great."

Tanner smiled as they stepped into the foyer. The pressure to win had always been there, but as the actual event got closer, it was squeezing harder.

"What are you two chatting about here, all by yourselves?" Keira found them, hooked her arm through Tanner's and pulled herself close to him.

"Business stuff," Quinn said, giving Keira and Tanner a broad smile. "But we're done here." He grew serious as he looked at Tanner. "Let me know later this week what you figure out."

Tanner nodded and as he left, Keira gave his arm a light jiggle, as if getting his attention. "What do you need to let him know?"

"Business stuff," Tanner repeated, giving her a quick smile. "So, what do you say we go for lunch? I thought we could go back to The Pasta Place. We could give them some support instead of the Grill and Chill for a change."

"Hopefully George won't find out."

"The competition is good for him. He needs to up his game if anything is going to happen between him and Brooke."

Keira stopped him with a finger on his mouth, her eyes wide with alarm. "Shush, you. It's the other way around."

Tanner was confused, but he wasn't going to waste any brain space on Brooke and George's puzzling relationship. Right now, he was enjoying Keira standing close to him. He caught her hand and kissed it, savoring the return to the easy give and take they always had as a couple.

"Let's go, then."

"I should let my parents know we won't be home for lunch," Keira said.

She pulled out her phone and while he waited for her to notify her parents, he got her coat. But just before he returned to the alcove where Keira stood, Alice came out of the church. Her eyes flicked from him to Keira's coat, hanging over his arm.

"Are you staying at the ranch tonight?" she asked.

"No. I'll be heading for Lethbridge. Why?"

"The carpenters need to talk to me about a bearing wall at the house. I was wondering if you could help me out."

For a moment Tanner felt torn. He recognized her appeal for help as another small connection she was trying to create.

"I can't until after the NFR," he said, acknowledging her request but not brushing it off completely. "If it can wait until then, I can help."

"That would be nice." She stood, watching him, as if she wanted to say something else, but then she turned and walked away.

As he watched her leave, pity for her brushed over his heart. She looked so alone. She had no husband, and her beloved son was dead. He was all she had left.

Which made him wonder if he should approach Alice about the ranch when he came back for Ellen's birthday.

Don't you want to wait until after the NFR?

But what if he didn't win?

He had to. Too much was riding on it. Literally.

"Hey, you, is that my coat?" Keira tugged at the coat he still held, and he turned his attention back to her.

"It is, my dear," he said, helping her put it on. As she zipped it up, he turned her around and pulled the hood up over her hair, taking a moment to brush a strand away from her face. Followed that with a gentle kiss.

He reminded himself that right now he was with Keira. The NFR and all it represented was a few days away yet.

For now, that was enough.

"WHEN WILL you be back for the birthday dinner?" Keira set her napkin down beside her plate, trying not to project her expectations on Tanner.

They were sitting in a quiet corner of The Pasta Place. It was an older institution. At one time it was run-down and fading but since the owner's daughter, Aubrey had come back, the place had been refurbished and the menu updated. It was cozy and had a lovely ambience.

Keira had come a couple of times with Brooke, but George at the Grill and Chill was a bigger draw for her friend.

"You just polished off a whole order of ravioli, two pieces of garlic toast, and a salad, and you want to talk about another meal?"

Tanner's crooked smile created a quiver in her stomach. He could always do that to her.

"No. I want to talk about family and being thankful for all the blessings we have."

He leaned forward and took her hands in his, his thumb caressing hers. "I have to go to Lethbridge tonight," he said, the reluctance in his voice sending a happy thrill through her. "I need to talk to my shop foreman face-to-face, but then I'll be back in time for the feast. If you're making your mom's infamous sweet potatoes, I'll be there."

"If that's all it takes, I'll make gallons of sweet potatoes. Plus, my dad had bought this fifteen-pound turkey that is going to take forever to stuff and even longer to eat," she added.

"I doubt I'd make that much of a dent in a turkey that size," he returned.

"I've seen you eat. You could definitely have an influence on the leftover quotient."

He laughed and once again Keira felt as if she had to pinch herself. To remind herself that this was Tanner sitting in front of her, not some figment of her imagination or a dream she would wake from.

"I'll be there as soon as I can," he said, grinning at her.

Keira nodded, holding his gaze, other questions rising to the surface.

After Tanner had kissed her the first time, she had made herself a promise that she wasn't going to think further ahead than the next moment with Tanner, but she couldn't stop the past and the future from slipping into the present.

"And then the NFR?" she said quietly.

Tanner drew in a long, slow breath, looking down at their joined hands. "Then the NFR. And after that..." He let his voice drift off as if he wasn't sure what was coming after that, either.

"Do you have to do this?" The question burst out of her before she could stop herself. Silly her. She wasn't just talking about some local rodeo. This was the Super Bowl of rodeos. What Tanner had been working toward all year.

But the thought of his motivation for competing burned like a sharp knife in her chest. Roger wasn't worth it.

Tanner's eyes narrowed a moment and the knife turned. Had she pushed him too hard? Asked too much?

"You know why I need to do this," he said quietly.

"But you're not doing it for yourself, are you?"

"It's all…laid out. All planned."

She heard an edge of desperation in his voice. As if he had to convince himself even more than he had to convince her.

"You make it sound as if you have no choice, but you do. You don't need to prove anything to anyone. Not anyone who matters."

"Alice matters."

Frustration clawed at her.

She wished she could tell him exactly why she wanted him to not compete. But she didn't dare say more.

Then he looked up at her and his smile was back, the warm intensity of his gaze making her cheeks flush.

"No matter what happens, I'm hoping that when I come back, we can be together."

Her shoulders dropped and the tightness in her neck eased. "I like the sound of that," she said quietly. It was enough, wasn't it?

Tanner's smile drifted off and he leaned forward, brushing a kiss over her lips as if to seal his promise. Then he sat back, his expression growing serious. "But that's the future. For now, we're here and I'm glad we could spend some time away from everyone else. It's been an interesting few days, hasn't it?" he asked quietly.

"A wonderful few days," Keira reiterated.

Tanner's smile shifted. "I never thought I would be able to say that I'm thankful for a good old-fashioned Alberta snowstorm."

Keira's only response was a warm smile. Then Tanner's expression grew serious again. "You know, I was hesitant to stop by the ranch when I first came here," he said quietly. "I brought the saddle other places but none of them could do it. I fought every inclination to come because I knew you were back, and I didn't want to face you again."

"Why was that?" she asked, though she knew precisely the

reason why he was. The precariousness of their growing relationship seemed to require going back over old ground in order to find their footing in this new place they had come to.

Tanner's grin showed her that he understood what she was doing, but it also showed her that he didn't seem to mind. As if he, too, understood the groundwork they needed to lay in order to move on.

"The thought of facing you made my heart hurt."

The blunt honesty of his response sent a stab of remorse through her and for a moment her own resolve wavered.

You need to tell him.

But she brushed the voice aside. Some events in the past needed to be dealt with but others were best left behind. They couldn't be changed.

"I'm sorry," she said quietly. "I sometimes wish we could go back and do things differently."

"How would you have?"

"I would have let you know what was important to me and what wasn't important so that you wouldn't think you had to do all that extra work just to provide for us. I think we should have talked more. I think we should have been more honest with each other. We didn't talk as much as we should have. We used to always pray and read the Bible together, but we lost that somewhere along the way."

"I know that was my fault," Tanner said quietly, looking down at their hands, now entwined. "After my dad died, I felt as if I lost my way. And then, when I found out I didn't get anything in his will, that hurt more than I wanted to admit, and I was too proud to tell you."

"And so it should. Have you ever found out why your dad did that?"

Tanner shook his head. "I think only Alice knows the real reason and we've not been especially close. And the only other person who could tell me was Dad, and he's gone."

Keira fought down the usual frustration over the situation then she stopped herself.

Forget the former things.

"And the lawyer?"

Tanner pulled his hands out of hers, folding his arms over his chest. His body language was eloquent, and Keira felt as if she had pushed things too far. Then he released a deep sigh. "I feel as if hiring this lawyer was part of what sent Roger to his death."

"That's crazy." The words burst out of Keira and as soon as she spoke them she wished she could take them back. Especially when a deep glower lowered Tanner's dark eyebrows, shading his eyes.

"Not crazy at all," he growled. "It was finding out about the lawyer that caused the fight between us. He was so angry with me." The pain in his voice cut like a knife.

"But that was Roger's problem, not yours," she said. "I've said it before and I'll say it again. It wasn't right for your father to do that regardless of your biology. You worked that ranch. You poured yourself into it. Besides, we don't know if it was Alice's idea or your father's. Maybe she had something over him. Some reason he did what he did."

Tanner's frown didn't bode well for the rest of the conversation, but she had started this, she felt she had to carry on.

"You have to stop taking on what you've been carrying the past few years. Roger's death had less to do with you hiring a lawyer than it had to do with the kind of person he was and the kind of choices he liked to make. You said yourself that he'd been drinking. You didn't put those drinks in his hand, and you didn't make him walk home. Roger had always been the kind of guy who did what he wanted and never cared about—" She stopped herself there. She was getting too emotional. The swarm of memories in her head rose. If she couldn't control them, they would come flying out.

She took a breath and stilled the storm.

Tanner plowed a hand through his hair, and he pushed out another sigh. "I know all that. I just don't think Alice does. I think, especially now, she feels like the ranch is her rightful heritage. I know I should have talked to her about it. Should have found out more. Seems too late now but maybe if I'd not been so proud, so angry, I would have confronted her."

And they were back to Alice again, but she shouldn't quibble. That was a safer topic than Roger.

Tanner picked up one of her hands and pressed a gentle kiss to it. "I know we should have talked about this before. Should have told you how I felt. What was going through my head and how I was planning to work around the problem of not inheriting the ranch. We were engaged and I should have talked to you about all of that. I'm sorry. So much happened because of what I didn't say. Maybe everything between us would be different. Maybe Roger wouldn't have died, and I wouldn't be tearing around the country, trying to balance rodeoing and running a business." His sigh came from deep within him and showed her how weary he was.

"You sound exhausted," she said quietly.

"I am. Part of me just wants to quit." He brushed another kiss over her hand. "Especially now. I feel like I have another focus since we got back together."

Tell him. Tell him. Maybe he won't go.

She felt the words beating in her chest. "Then quit. Stay home."

The gentle shake of Tanner's head shot down the idea. "I'm so close. I would feel like all the sacrifices I made the past year would be worth nothing if I stopped now." He smiled at her again. "And you, working on Roger's saddle, gave us time together. I feel like it kind of wove everything from our past into our present."

The wings beat harder.

"Though I feel like quitting, it's just one more weekend," Tanner continued. "And when it's done, I hope I can come back to the ranch and give Alice Roger's saddle and the trophy. Maybe I'm a dreamer but I'm hoping it will give her a reason to forgive me. And, I guess, I'm hoping it will give me some peace. Finish what he started and lay his memory to rest."

Keira clung to his hands, looking down at them, tracing their familiar scars and marks. Hands that had held her, taught her how to hold the reins, carried her through swollen spring streams, and held out a diamond ring to her when he had asked her to marry him.

Her heart plunged with a sudden pain.

"Do you think Roger would do the same for you?" she asked, deliberately leaching her voice of emotion. "If your situations were reversed?"

The sudden narrowing of his eyes showed her words hit a chord.

"Maybe not," he admitted, tightening his grip on her hands. "And maybe that's another reason I need to win this title."

"To show you're the better man?"

He slowly shook his head and then he released a hard laugh. "You always had that uncanny ability to get to the heart of a matter. To see stuff I couldn't." He shrugged slowly as if letting the idea settle and take root. "Maybe that's been part of my reasoning. The part I never wanted to look at too closely."

"You are the better man, you know," Keira said quietly, squeezing his hands harder. Tighter, praying he would be convinced. "You always were."

"Well, I guess we'll see if I am the better rider."

She gave it one more shot, knowing that her reasons were selfish but also knowing she needed to try one more time.

"You don't need to prove that, either. Stay here after our dinner. Let go of the burden. Alice will think what she thinks."

"This matters a lot to you. Why?"

Tell him. Tell him.

But she couldn't. Things were too fragile, and she didn't want to risk rupturing their faint connection. They were just rebuilding the foundation of their relationship.

It was too soon.

CHAPTER ELEVEN

anner pulled up beside Monty's truck, turned off the engine and gave himself a moment to gather his thoughts. Enjoy the utter quiet of the ranch after the steady drone of his truck engine.

His ears buzzed and his head ached and too many thoughts paraded through his brain, each demanding attention. He was excited to see Keira, but that was now tempered by the events of the past few days.

Quinn's conversation with him had buzzed around the back of his head, adding to the juggling of plans he was doing. Alice would need someone to take care of the ranch.

Why not him?

And why should you be leasing a place you worked on as a kid?

He pushed the questions aside, got out of the truck, placed his hands in the small of his back and stretched out the kinks gathered from four hours of tense driving.

Then shivered as a winter breeze tugged at his hair. He reached into the truck and pulled his hat out, dropped it on his head, then grabbed his overnight bag from behind the seat of his truck. He was going to repack it, put it back in the truck so he could leave first thing tomorrow morning for Vegas.

Apprehension shivered through him at the thought. Tomorrow already.

He looked back at the ranch house, a cap of snow on its roof catching the rays of the setting sun. Keira was there, waiting. They had called each other every night, just to talk. He missed her. How would he be able to leave tomorrow?

"How was your trip back to the office?"

Monty's voice behind him gave Tanner a start. He turned to Monty and grinned.

"Aren't you cold?" he returned.

The older man wore a down-filled jacket, but it was open, his gloves stuffed in the pocket, his head bare.

"It's a balmy day today compared to yesterday's wind and drifting snow," Monty said with a grin. "Is everything running smoothly at the shop?"

Tanner picked up his bag and shook his head, frustration and worry gripping him again. "Not really. I knew I was pushing my luck being gone as long as I had. It's not going well."

That was an understatement.

Though he'd stayed in constant touch with his shop foreman and had received good reports from him, his visit showed that quality control had slipped in the week and a half he'd been gone. The tools were in disarray. A couple of disgruntled customers had called him while he was on the road to tell him how unhappy they were with the work. Tanner had to promise that the work would be redone free of charge. The balance sheet had been precarious this year because he'd been gone too much, but the past week had created a tipping point. "I've been neglecting the business too much the past six months. I need to spend more time there."

"But you came back here, anyway?"

"I got things sorted out for now. Once the NFR is done..."

He let the sentence trail off as the questions that had haunted him the past week revisited.

"What happens after that?"

Tanner knew that Monty was thinking of Keira. As was he.

He looked past Monty to the mountains, now pristine white against a bright blue sky. Sharp, brilliant colors and silent open spaces. His heart ached to be back here.

"I used to think I would go back to Lethbridge and get back to work. But I'm not sure anymore."

Monty sighed, then zipped up his coat and slipped on his gloves. "You belong here, you know."

"In more ways than one," Tanner said quietly, thinking of Keira. His heart ached to be with her even more than it did to be back in the valley. "But I need to make a living and I couldn't figure out how to do it after Dad died. Running that garage is the only thing I've got going for me now."

"You're a good mechanic, Tanner, but you're a rancher from your boots up."

"A rancher without a ranch." Tanner couldn't help the bitter note. He had struggled for so long with what his father had done. In fact, at times, he thought he had made his peace with it. But now all the old emotions came back.

Monty hunched his shoulders against a chill that was slowly making itself felt through the thin layers of the jacket Tanner had worn while driving. It seemed Monty wasn't in any hurry to get to the house. Tanner sensed he had more to say.

Monty blew out a sigh, his breath a cloud of white vapor in the chilly air. "I don't want to be nosy, but I sense things are building between you and Keira." He held up his hand as if to forestall anything Tanner might have to say to that. "And I don't want to make all kinds of assumptions, but I think you need to talk to Alice. About the ranch. Not for Keira's sake, but for your own."

His words fell between them, bringing another harsh reality

into the moment. The future and Keira and how that would look.

"I guess I had hoped to do that after the NFR," Tanner said, shifting his bag to his other hand. "I had hoped to come to her with Roger's saddle and some kind of trophy. Then see where the conversation takes us."

"You'd only have a trophy if you won."

"I'm confident I'll at least place. I just heard that Brad Butler, my strongest competitor, just bowed out. He busted his ankle this past weekend."

"Rodeoing?"

"No. Snowboarding. What self-respecting cowboy snowboards anyhow?" he asked with a laugh. "So, I'm reasonably confident. Have to be."

Monty held his gaze, his eyes piercing. "What your father did wasn't right," he said, echoing what Keira had told him again and again. "Your grandfather started that ranch and worked it to where it is now. Now, just so you know, I got nothing against Alice personally. She's a good friend to Ellen and has taken excellent care of her the past few weeks, but what Alice is doing isn't right, either. That ranch belongs as much to you and any kids you might have. I know she had hoped that Roger would take it over but we both know that even if he were still alive, he wouldn't have stayed on the ranch. It wasn't in his blood like it's in yours. Ranching is your identity."

And Tanner's thoughts immediately bounced back to Keira and the feelings growing between them.

"Now, like I said, I don't know what exactly is going on between you and my daughter," Monty continued, as if reading Tanner's mind, his tone growing serious, "but I know she's had some hard times."

"It was Keira who broke off the engagement," Tanner reminded Monty. "Not me."

Monty laid his hand on Tanner's shoulder, his expression

holding a hint of sorrow. "I know, son. I'm not blaming you. I just know that after she broke up with you it was as if she lost a part of herself. Something vital. She was an anxious and uptight girl when she came back from Edmonton, but she's found peace here. She belongs here, too." He was quiet a moment, as if letting his comment settle and take root, then slapped his gloved hands together. "But enough of that. I don't want to throw anything more on your shoulders. And I better get inside, though I'll probably get roped into doing some kind of decorating thing. Girls have been busy like crazy the past couple days getting ready for Ellen's party."

He took a step away, then turned back to Tanner. "And talk to Alice. Before or after the NFR, your choice. But you need to find a way to make this right."

Monty's words rang in Tanner's head as he walked back to the bunkhouse. Tanner wasn't sure what the outcome would be of any discussion he could have with Alice or why it should fall on his shoulders to do so, but at the same time he felt as if circumstances were pushing him toward that conversation.

He dropped his bag off in the bunkhouse, stopped in the bathroom a moment to freshen up. He sorted through the clothes he had taken back with him from Lethbridge. Got his chaps ready and quickly repacked his bag and set out the case that held his rigging. When he had gone to Lethbridge, he'd picked up his old saddle as a backup. Just in case something happened to Roger's. He hoped he didn't need it, but it didn't hurt to have an extra.

All he needed was Roger's saddle and he was ready to go.

Should have taken the time to practice, he thought, but pushed the idea away. He was as ready as he could be. From here on in everything else was out of his control.

Ten minutes later his truck was packed up and he was striding across the yard, heading to the ranch house, his heart quickening with each step closer to Keira.

An old cream can sat just inside the porch of the house stuffed with cattails and branches. They looked out of place with the snow piling against the window behind it, but it was a cheery touch.

Tanner took off his boots, his heart lifting at the sound of Keira's voice, of footsteps hurrying to the door.

And then there she was. Her hair hanging loose around her shoulders, her eyes bright, her smile wide as the Alberta sky.

"Hey, there," she said, stopping in the doorway, as if unsure of what to do next.

Tanner shook off his coat, swept off his hat, closed the distance between them in two large strides and pulled her into his arms. He held her tight, breathing in the smell of her perfume, feeling, for the first time since he'd pulled onto the ranch, that he had come home.

He pulled away from her and brushed her hair back from her face.

"Hey, you," he said quietly. "I missed you."

Keira bracketed his face with her hands, her smile growing incandescent. "I missed you, too."

He kissed her once, then again. He truly felt as if he had come home as he looked deep into her eyes. Though questions remained, he believed that they didn't matter as long as they had each other.

Then as he slipped his arm around her, they turned to walk into the kitchen.

Alice stood by the counter, rolling out pie dough. She looked up when he came in; her eyes flicking from him to Keira then back to him again.

The moment of peace was edged away by the disapproval in her expression and the downward drift of her lips.

He thought of what Monty had encouraged him to do even as he clung to Keira beside him.

Keira was the reason he had to talk to Alice about his future.

He just prayed it would turn out well.

"WELL, Ellen, I think we're going to have to delay your birthday dinner every year. I think that's the best supper I've ever had," Monty exclaimed, wiping his mouth with the cloth napkin that Keira had so carefully folded only an hour ago. "Though I don't think I've ever sat down to such a fancy table since we moved here." He gave Keira a benevolent smile, which she returned, thankful for his praise, but even more thankful for the man sitting beside her.

Because they had missed Ellen's birthday, Keira was determined that they celebrate it in style. So, she had laid out the linen tablecloth and matching napkins she had purchased on a trip to Calgary she and Brooke had taken on Monday. The fancy china for special occasions had been taken out and laid on gold-coloured chargers that Keira had also purchased. Then Keira had made two centerpieces of pink and yellow mums accented with white roses, all set off with sage green eucalyptus leaves. Ellen had said she didn't want a fuss, but Keira could tell that she was tickled. They were set out on the table interspersed with candles of varying heights, creating a festive air. The lights had been lowered and a feeling of peace and tranquility had descended over the dining room.

The only "off" note was Alice. While they were working together on the meal, Alice had been pleasant and helpful, though somewhat subdued. Then, when Tanner came, Alice withdrew into herself, became quiet and, Keira sensed, disapproving. All through the meal, Alice seemed to grow more uptight by the minute, which surprised Keira. She thought that Tanner's devoting this year to Roger had eased away the tension between them.

But today she sensed it was back and stronger than ever.

"Another piece of pie, Keira?" Alice was asking, holding up the pie plate still half full of pumpkin pie.

"It was delicious, but no thanks," Keira said, placing her hand on her full stomach. She knew she shouldn't have had that last piece, but Alice had insisted. And for the sake of trying to maintain a semblance of peace with Alice, she had given in.

Tanner, his arm draped over her shoulders, scoffed at her. "What?" he asked, squeezing her shoulder with his hand. "You only had two pieces. The Keira I know and love isn't such a lightweight."

Know and love was just a saying, she knew that, but she couldn't stop her heart from leaping at the words.

She slanted him a teasing grin. "Call me a lightweight again and you'll be facing me across a game of Scrabble."

"Wonderful idea," Ellen said, carefully wiping her mouth with a napkin. Though she still had to be careful what she ate, this meal she had managed to eat a bite of turkey and some stuffing. "This time, though, we'll play by my rules, not yours."

"But our rules are more fun," Tanner said.

Ellen gave them a benevolent smile, and for Keira's, Monty's, and Ellen's obvious happiness at what was growing between her and Tanner mitigated Alice's veiled hostility.

Though Keira knew even more than they did what was happening, she hardly dared take it in. Yesterday she had been unable to concentrate on her leather work, wondering if Tanner would come back for their postponed dinner. Would he be able to take the time away from his business?

Last night he had called, telling her that he would probably be late. He'd had some trouble at the shop he'd had to clear up. She had tried not to worry at the tense tone in his voice, the frustration that he barely masked. After their terse phone call, she'd called Freya. Thankfully her husband, Cody, was working in the shop so she was alone. Together they'd gone over all the nuances of her conversation with Tanner.

Freya had encouraged her. Told her that Tanner looked happy. Content. That they belonged together.

Keira had come so close to telling Freya everything. Each day with Tanner it was like the old secret she had held close was inching to the surface. She tried to push it down, but it kept rising. Her dear friend never knew though she had come very close to telling her.

But now, if she told anyone, it had to be Tanner.

All day she'd listened for the sound of his truck, her emotions veering between worry and hope. When he finally came, her restless, yearning heart settled; she felt suddenly complete.

"Hey, Latigo Kid," he said quietly, the familiar goofy endearment making her heart give a little flip. She shifted so she could get closer to him, quietly thanking the Lord for this moment. For this man.

You must tell him.

Ice slipped through her veins at the unexpected and unwelcome return of the pernicious voice. She pushed it back, willing it away, trying to bury it.

But it lingered like a malevolent shadow just over her shoulder, waiting, watching. It had been growing of late, that voice. The closer she got to Tanner, the stronger it grew.

She clenched her hands into tight fists and Tanner, ever aware of each shift in her mood, bent his head closer to her.

"Everything okay?" he asked, his soft-spoken words holding a trace of concern.

She flashed him a smile and settled against him. "Yeah. It's all good," she said.

But the shadow lingered.

"I thought we could read from Psalm ninety-five for our after-supper devotion. A nod to my dear wife," Monty said. "I know it's your favorite one."

Ellen just smiled, sitting back in her chair. Monty had given a warm speech before dinner, telling everyone how much he loved his wife and how thankful he was for her presence.

Keira had teared up listening to him, trying not to think ahead to her birthday. Wonder if she and Tanner would celebrate it together.

Monty picked up the Bible from the sideboard, where it always resided. He returned to the table and opened it to the marked spot. He slipped his reading glasses on and then took a moment to look around the table. "I know that this past year has had its difficulties, and while this isn't Ellen's actual birthday, this is our own particular time to celebrate her life." He glanced at Ellen, still sitting stiffly in her neck brace, and gave her a gentle smile, then turned to Alice. "Ellen and I are both thankful you could be here to help us, Alice. Of course, we're sad that Heather and Lee couldn't be here, and we continue to pray for them..." His voice trailed off a moment and Keira had to swallow down her own sorrow, as well. She had written Heather and texted Lee but both had clearly stated they couldn't come. Both had given work as the reason and in Lee's case, Keira suspected it was true. He'd had difficulty finding a job after his years in jail, so she suspected he didn't want to jeopardize his standing with the company he had finally found work with. But in Heather's situation, Keira suspected something else was going on because even before the storm changed all the plans, Heather had said that she might not be coming for Ellen's birthday no matter when it was held. And Christmas was still uncertain.

The thought made her sad and Keira leaned just a little closer to Tanner, who seemed to sense her sorrow and gently stroked her shoulder.

Monty cleared his throat and then gave Keira and Tanner the benefit of his smile. "But we are also thankful for the gifts God has given us and thankful for Keira and..." He paused a moment, as if unsure if he should put his daughter and Tanner together yet. But he recovered. "And we are also thankful to have Tanner with us." Then he adjusted his glasses, looked down and started reading.

"*Come, let us sing for joy to the Lord; let us shout aloud to the Rock of our salvation. Let us come before Him with thanksgiving and extol Him with music and song. For the Lord is the great God, the great King above all gods.*"

Keira let the words of the passage her father was reading wash over her weary soul. God was her rock and had been through the turbulent times of her life. And, He had brought Tanner back into her life. She didn't dare think too far ahead yet, but for now, she was thankful.

She glanced sidelong at Tanner to connect with him, but was surprised to see him looking at Alice, a faint frown tugging at his eyebrows. But Alice wasn't looking at him at all. Instead, her head was lowered, her eyes focused on her hands folded on the table, lips pressed tightly together.

Then, to Keira's surprise and consternation, she saw the shining track of a tear slide down her face.

Her heart softened a moment as she reminded herself that despite what Roger was, he was still Alice's beloved son. And she didn't have him anymore.

"*For He is our God, and we are the people of His pasture, the flock under His care.*" Monty paused at the end of the reading, then closed the Bible and eased out a sigh.

"I think it's important to remind ourselves that we are truly under God's care. That He does watch over us and has a purpose for our lives. That He spared Ellen's life for a reason and for which I'm so incredibly thankful." Monty gave his wife a warm smile and she returned it.

Then he set the Bible on the table and looked around at the gathering. "So, in light of that, I was wondering if we could talk about how God has worked in our lives the past while and maybe mention things we are thankful for."

Monty paused a moment, to let the idea settle, then turned to Ellen, holding her hand in his. "So, I know you're not in the best place right now, my dear, but I know that I've learned a lot about being thankful in all circumstances from you."

Gratitude permeated Keira's soul at the sight of her parents' obvious love for each other. They had been through a lot the past few years. Lee's accident and subsequent time in jail. Heather marrying a man they didn't approve of and her moving to New York with him. Now Ellen's accident. Yet, through it all their love for each other was obvious to any who knew them.

"I struggle with thankfulness, but I know I am thankful that we could be here together," Ellen said, granting Keira a warm smile, her gaze taking in Tanner, as well. "I'm also happy Tanner could be here with us and that you two are together again."

Together again.

The words, spoken aloud by her mother, seemed to make the relationship suddenly tangible and real.

"I'm thankful for a lot of things, too," Tanner said, looking down at Keira again. "It's been a long hard road, but it brought me back here and for that, I thank our Lord." Then he looked across the table at Alice. "And I must add that I'm grateful I could spend the last few weeks with you, Alice. It means a lot to be here, together."

Alice looked up at that, blinking as if to get rid of the tears she had just struggled through. "I appreciate that," she said quietly. "And I look forward to seeing you compete with Roger's saddle. I know that will make the past two years easier to bear."

Keira tried not to let the woman's expectations of Tanner weigh her down, but she felt as if an extra burden was suddenly placed on his shoulders. He carried enough guilt over Roger; Alice's expectations only seemed to add to the burden.

He shouldn't be carrying this, and you know why.

Keira pressed her lips together, her hands clenched as she pushed the voice back where it belonged. Down. Buried.

"And because of Keira's hard work, Roger's saddle is now finished," Tanner continued. "I'm as ready to go as I can be."

"When do you leave?" Alice asked.

"Tomorrow."

"Do you think you can do it?" Strangely, Alice seemed confrontational.

What was wrong with her? And why was she glaring at Tanner as if she was angry with him? She knew Alice blamed Tanner for Roger's death, but from the way Alice had been acting the past few days, Keira thought she'd gotten through that by now. Especially with Tanner devoting this past year to his brother.

"Tanner is a good rider. One of the best," Keira said, feeling the need to defend him. "Of course he can do it."

Alice's gaze snapped to Keira. "You of all people should know he was never as good as Roger."

Keira clenched her fists under the table, holding Alice's gaze look for look, anger and a myriad of other emotions whirling through her. How could she say something like that, especially right in front of her son? "Tanner's the best man I know."

Alice's eyes widened. "How can you say that? You know Roger was the better man in so many ways. I warned him not to date you. That he was just a rebound romance for you, but he said he loved you. That he wanted to marry you." Her staccato words were like shots to Keira's heart.

Keira heard Tanner's gasp as her thoughts spun and whirled like a dark vortex. What was Alice saying? Her heart threatened to thunder in her chest. She had it wrong. So terribly wrong.

"I never... Roger was never..." Her voice choked off. She couldn't speak. Couldn't think. She swallowed back words that clamored to be spoken.

She had to leave.

"Excuse me," she said, making every effort to keep her voice even. Steady.

CAROLYNE AARSEN

"Are you okay? Do you want me to come with you?" Tanner asked, rising to his feet.

She shook her head, laying her hand on his shoulder, exerting every ounce of willpower as she struggled to maintain her composure. "We'll talk later, I promise," she said quietly. "Please, just give me a few moments alone. Please."

She ignored Tanner's look of concern, her parents' puzzlement, and Alice's piercing gaze and, eyes downcast, she walked out of the room, willing herself not to rush.

She made her way to the bathroom, closed the door and, leaning against it, slid down to the floor.

She grabbed her head, lowering her forehead to her upraised knees.

"Please, Lord," was all she could say. She had to pull it together. She couldn't fall apart now.

CHAPTER TWELVE

$\mathcal{T}$anner watched Keira leave, his own emotions in turmoil as his stepmother's words rang like a hammer through his head.

Roger had wanted to *marry* Keira? She hadn't told him any of that. Though she had asked for a moment alone, he couldn't stop from pushing his chair back to follow her. To find out more.

"I'm sorry for what I said," Alice said to Ellen and Monty, thankfully acknowledging how inappropriate her previous comments were. "I'm feeling too emotional right now."

Tanner looked back, still feeling torn.

"If you don't mind, I'd like a word with Tanner?" Alice continued, getting up from the table.

It was the pleading tone in her voice that drew his attention away from Keira, walking down the hallway away from him, back to his stepmother.

"I need to talk to you," Alice continued. "As soon as possible."

Tanner felt torn, but knew he had to give Keira the space she asked for. He would talk to her later.

Alice looked to Ellen and Monty and laid a gentle hand on

Ellen's shoulder. "Again, I'm sorry, but I need to talk to Tanner in private. I'll take care of the dishes when I come back. Please, don't do any of it. I can't have you cleaning up your birthday dinner."

"Don't worry about the cleanup," Ellen said. "You do what you need to do. It can wait."

It wasn't hard to hear the strained note in Ellen's voice, and Tanner understood where she was coming from. He was still trying to absorb the shock of what Alice had just dumped on them. He could only imagine what was going through Monty's and Ellen's minds.

"Use my office," Monty said, getting up from the table. "You can talk in private there."

Alice nodded at his gracious offer and, without a backward glance at Tanner to see if he was following, walked in the opposite direction Keira had gone, to the room just off the living room.

Tanner headed after her and closed the door of Monty's office behind him, leaning against it as if to support himself. Alice stopped by the desk, her hands woven together.

"Did Roger really want to marry Keira?" was the first thing out of his mouth as his mother turned to face him.

"He loved her," was all Alice said, taking on the melancholy tone that was her default emotion whenever she talked of Roger. "When they dated, it was all he talked about. How he wanted to make Keira his wife and live on the ranch."

Tanner fisted his hands to keep his emotions in check. He had a hard time believing his stepmother, and yet his thoughts shifted to the confession Keira had made about dating Roger after she broke up with him.

Had something more happened between her and Roger that would make his stepbrother hope they would get married?

He tried to dismiss the idea, but it clung, pernicious and evil as his thoughts rushed backward. How Roger had changed after that summer Keira left. How despondent he had become. How much more he started to drink.

"Another thing we need to talk about is Keira."

Alice's voice came from a faraway place and Tanner blinked, trying to bring himself from past into present.

"What do you mean, talk about Keira?"

"I know you and Keira have a history. But I hope you don't let her distract you. When you told me that you were dedicating this season to Roger, it felt right. Going to the National Finals was a dream of Roger's from the first moment Cyrus put him in a saddle. He came so close the year...the year he died." Alice released a heavy sigh and leaned back against Monty's desk, her hand resting on the edge, as if the weight of the memories was too much for her to hold up on her own. "To hear you say that you want to finish what your brother started means the world to me. I'm so sorry for what I said about you not being man that Roger was. I was hurt and angry. It bothered...bothers me to see you with Keira, that was why I got upset and said what I did. I need you to know that I'm proud of what you're doing in memory of Roger."

She wasn't his mother and had made that clear from an early age. But to hear her say she was proud of him created an unexpected lightness. For the first time in many years, he dared nurture a faint hope that she might see him as more than a stepson.

"Thank you." He chose to ignore her comment about Keira. That could be dealt with another time.

"But in order to finish what you start, you need to stay focused," Alice continued, her eyes now blazing with intensity. "You're close. I know you are. I checked the standings and you're very high. But you can't let Keira distract you."

Resentment flashed through him both at how proprietary she had become with something she had found out only a couple of weeks ago and how she presumed to tell him what to do about Keira. "I know what I need to do," he said, his tone careful and measured, trying not to let her pressure get to him.

"That's good. And I think you know that Roger would be proud of you, too." She smiled, satisfied as she pushed away from the desk. As if her job was done.

"Before I leave for Vegas," he said, forestalling her exit. "There's something else we need to discuss."

As he pulled in a deep breath, his heart kicked up a few notches. A lot rode on the next few moments—and her reaction. He prayed for strength and that she would understand.

"I'd like to talk to you about the ranch."

Alice turned the corners of her mouth down, folded her arms over her chest. "What about the ranch?"

Tanner forced himself to look directly at Alice and hold her frowning gaze. Not to back down. He wasn't afraid of her, but he was afraid of the consequences should she turn him down.

"I'd like to run it. I'd like to find a way to buy it from you."

Alice sucked in her breath, but her eyes flicked away from him. "You're thinking of moving back here?"

"I'd like to. I grew up here. Grew up on the Circle C. All my best memories are there. I miss working cattle and I miss...I miss being with Keira."

Alice drummed her fingers on her arm, also not a good sign. She would do that whenever he or Roger had done something she was unhappy with, and she was deciding on the best punishment to mete out.

"How do you propose to pay for the ranch? I've been offered a lot of money for it."

As he had since his father died, Tanner had to work hard to keep his emotions out of the situation. He shouldn't have to buy his father's ranch back, but he kept those thoughts at bay. One step at a time. "I was hoping you would realize that while Cyrus wasn't my biological father, he was my father. I worked the ranch my entire life. I had hoped he would have created an equitable way for me to buy into it."

"But he willed it to me. Roger was his biological son." Her words were crisp, her tone sharp, defensive.

"I know that. But surely you must realize how this looked to me after all the work I did here. I didn't know my biological father. Cyrus was the only one I had. I thought he would take care of me. Not favor Roger over all I had done."

"I know you've always resented my place in your life," Alice interrupted him, shifting the conversation back to herself.

Tanner held his hand up to stop this line of thinking. "I was only five when my father married you. You were the only mother I ever knew. My father married you for a reason. I know he must have loved you." Tanner threw the words out, hoping something would connect. The fights that went on in the house when he was old enough to understand were hardly indicative of a loving relationship, but something must have drawn his father to Alice for him to marry her.

Alice slumped against the desk again, her fingers worrying at the hem of her pale blue sweater. "He did. At first." She stopped there and Tanner heard genuine pain in her voice and his anger with her softened. A bit.

"But regardless of your past relationship with my father," he continued, "you've got to understand where I'm coming from. My dad willing his ranch to you and you not recognizing me in any way hurt more than I think you realize regardless of blood."

Tanner hoped to appeal to some sense of fair play. It was the only leverage he had right now.

"I'd like to negotiate something with you," he said. "I'd like to come back to the area and start a life here."

"And what about your mechanic shop? I helped you out when you had to buy it. You got some of the money from the ranch through that."

Tanner released a sharp breath. Yes, Alice had helped him,

but the ten thousand she gave him was a pittance compared to what the ranch was worth. "And I've always appreciated that. But working there was never my dream. Not like ranching."

She fiddled with the hem of her sweater, then pulled in a deep breath, stiffened her spine, and looked directly at him, steely resolve turning her eyes into flint.

"Why don't we talk about this later. After the finals in Vegas. I know people don't think it's right that I got the ranch, and I want to be fair about it. But for now, let's first lay Roger's soul to rest, shall we? After the Finals, we'll talk."

Tanner could only nod as a chill entered his soul. His past mistakes had been enough to carry him into the finals. Now his future was added to that burden, as well?

"That's all I can ask for," he said quietly. "For now, I need to go talk to Keira."

Alice's lips tightened at the mention of her name but thankfully she didn't say anything more. Tanner left the room, but Keira wasn't in the kitchen when he returned. Monty and Ellen were making a valiant attempt at cleaning up and as Alice entered the kitchen, she reprimanded them and took over.

"If you're looking for Keira, she went out to the shop," Ellen said to Tanner as she set a stack of dishes on the island by the dishwasher. "You go talk to her. We can finish up here."

Tanner didn't need any further encouragement, but the note of concern in Ellen's voice gave him added impetus. He hurried to the porch, grabbed his jacket and threaded his hands through the sleeves as he tried to jam his feet into his boots. Urgency made him clumsy and slowed his movements.

Finally, he was out the door, the wan light of the shop casting a glow over the shoveled walkway.

The door of the shop was ajar, and he heard Keira's quiet voice and he realized she was talking to Sugar.

"I don't know what to do," she said, the plaintiveness in her voice tearing at his soul. She sounded lost. Alone.

Scared.

But why?

Help me through this, Lord, he prayed, not sure what else to do. Then he pushed open the door, its squeak echoing through the quiet of the shop.

Keira sat on the floor, her back resting against the workbench, stroking Sugar's head, who was curled up beside her.

Both Sugar and Keira looked up at Tanner as he closed the door behind him. Neither got up, as if they'd known he was coming. As he came closer Tanner's heartbeat faltered at the sight of Keira's face. Her eyes were red-rimmed and haunted. Her features looked as if they had been dragged down.

"What's wrong?" he asked, dropping to her side, sliding his arm around her shoulders.

She resisted a moment, then drifted into him, her head resting on his shoulder.

"We need to talk."

Four words no man ever wanted to hear. Tanner sent up another prayer and waited. And for the second time this evening, feeling as if far too much was riding on this moment.

"Sorry I took off on you," Keira whispered, letting the warmth of Tanner's shoulder seep into her. Her forehead felt tight, and her cheeks were hot, but inside she felt cold as ice.

Tanner took her hand in his. It was warm and completely enfolded hers. She heard his ragged sigh, and she waited a moment longer, allowing herself this moment of calm before everything between them changed.

"That's okay," Tanner said. "I guessed Alice upset you. I would have come after you, but she needed to talk to me."

"What about?" Keira knew her inane question was simply

putting off the inevitable, but she couldn't simply jump into this.

"The ranch. If all goes well at the NFR, she said she would consider finding a way to make it mine when I come back from Vegas." He clasped her hand just a bit tighter. "Which I'm excited about. Because that will mean I can think about a future. Here. In the valley."

In his voice she heard a hope that both excited her and sent her heart spiraling downward. Would they have a future?

"What did you need to say to me?" he asked. "In the house you said we would talk later."

Keira felt as if she stood on the edge of a precipice, teetering, struggling to hold her balance. Once she released the words there was no taking them back. They would be out in the world. Real. Alive.

She closed her eyes, clinging to Tanner's hand, praying for strength and courage.

"It's about Roger..." She faltered, wishing she didn't have to have this conversation but knowing that if they were going to move into the future that she hoped they might have, this needed to be dealt with.

Tanner stiffened, dropping her hands. Creating a distance that chipped away at her resolve.

"Did you want to *marry* him?" he said with narrowed eyes and clenched teeth.

Keira grabbed his shoulder, praying he believed her. "No. Never. Roger was delusional. I never wanted to marry him. Ever." She spoke with force, clinging to her anger to control her fear.

"I'm glad," was all Tanner said. His displeasure faded away as he stroked her face. "I'm having a hard enough time with my memories of Roger. I didn't need that added to the mix."

Keira's heart turned over, her breath quickened, and she sent up a scattered prayer for strength.

"That summer, after I broke up with you…" Her voice trailed off as she forced herself into the past. "It was hard. I knew I'd a made a mistake. I wanted to get back together with you, but I also knew how proud you can be." She shifted away from him, wrapping her arms around her knees, but thankfully, he kept his arm around her shoulders.

"I was mixed up and confused, and then Roger was home and he invited me to a party with him. I went and we had fun and I asked about you and he told me a few things about you. How you'd placed first in the past two rodeos. How you were getting money together. He told me about your work as a mechanic. I was hungry for anything I could find out about you."

"Why didn't you talk to me, ask me?" The hurt in his voice was palpable but she couldn't dwell on that. She had to stick with the facts. It was the only way to get through all of this.

"I'm a proud person, too," she said, tightening her grip on her knees. "I'd broken up with you and I wasn't ready to forgive you for not being able to stay in the valley. I didn't think I had any right to contact you. And then the third time Roger and I went out he told me about the will, and I understood better why you were working so hard. But he…he also told me about girls you were dating—"

"What? I never dated any girls."

She shot him a puzzled glance, surprised at his anger. "He said you went out every night when you guys were on the road. That you always had girls with you."

"Not because I asked them, and I certainly didn't date any of them." Tanner's eyebrows were dark slashes over eyes burning with an indignation that both exhilarated and frightened her. "They were just girls who liked to hang around cowboys after a rodeo. Buckle bunnies. Groupies. Whatever you want to call them."

"So, Roger was lying."

"Absolutely."

The conviction in his voice thrilled her but at the same time she felt a growing tempest of fury rising in her. Roger... He'd done too much damage.

She sucked in a deep breath, struggling to stay on top of the storm brewing, a storm that had been always latent but now was seeping through the fissures of her slowly eroding self-control.

"I'm guessing, though, you didn't want to talk to me just about the lies my stepbrother had been feeding you." Tanner's voice was gentle, but she sensed the steel behind it.

Another breath. Another prayer.

"That summer, Roger and I went out a bunch of times," she said, floundering through all of this. "When he told me about the...dates...I was angry. Upset. Even though I'd broken up with you, I missed you. I knew I had made a mistake and if I'd known exactly why you were so busy, if we'd talked more...maybe... maybe everything would have been different." She paused, teetering, then pushed on. "Roger and I went to a party one night. It was a bush party and it got wild. I was upset and not thinking straight." She leached all the emotion out of her voice, bringing the conversation to a simple recitation of the facts. "I had too much to drink. So did Roger. He tried to make out with me and for a little while I let him. Then I told him to stop. That I didn't want it and wasn't over you. I drank some more and then, of course, went out to the bushes to get sick, and he found me there. He tried to help me, and I told him I was fine. He insisted and I got mad at him. Told him to leave me alone. I was still upset with what he told me. Then he grabbed me and told me to get over you. That you were totally over me. That you didn't care about me. That you were glad I broke up the engagement because you were looking for an excuse to break up with me, anyway."

Tanner's gasp registered on some level, but she plunged on.

"He grabbed me and tried to kiss me again. I pushed him away and he got angry. Told me I had been leading him on. That he'd always liked me and knew I always liked him."

She heard her own voice grow flat, even and monotone as she dealt out the facts like cards from a deck.

"He kissed me, and I told him not to. He began pulling on my hair, grabbing it. I pulled away, tried to run away but he caught me. Then I tried to fight him off, but he was stronger than me. He threw me down on the ground and then he—"

"Please stop."

Tanner's voice resounded like a shot in the shop. Keira flinched, but stayed where she was, staring blindly ahead, seeing only the vivid memories that she had kept suppressed so long, now flooding her mind.

Tanner jerked away from her and jumped to his feet, pacing back and forth in front of her.

She stayed where she was, reminding herself what Dana, her counselor in Edmonton, had told her again and again.

I didn't ask for it. It's not my fault.

But the anger rolling off Tanner as he strode back and forth in front of her, keeping his distance, detonated doubts and second thoughts. Did he believe her? Did he think she asked for it?

What did you expect? You throw this bomb at him about the brother who he would do anything for. Did you think he would wrap his arms around you and tell you that it's all okay? That all is forgiven? You're not the sweet innocent girl he proposed to?

She slowly got to her feet, her movements wooden and stiff. She couldn't look at him because she didn't want to see the condemnation in his face. Didn't want to see his disappointment and his anger. How often hadn't he told her how much he loved her innocence?

Not so innocent anymore.

She walked slowly to the hook that held her coat, Sugar right at her heels. She pulled her coat off the hook and slipped it on, her hands clumsy, her movements uncoordinated.

All the while Tanner kept a distance between them. It was only a few feet, but it may as well have been a yawning chasm. He didn't want her anymore. How could he?

She shot a quick glance at him and then said, "I think you better go."

Without another word, she pulled her hood up, tugged open the door and, with her faithful companion, Sugar, trotting behind her, left the shop.

Left Tanner.

It was over.

CHAPTER THIRTEEN

*H*e couldn't think. Couldn't process. Thoughts, reactions, memories clashed in his mind, a fierce battle he couldn't control.

Roger. With Keira.

Lies and mistruths and devastation.

Roger. Hurting Keira.

He hadn't let her finish her story, but he didn't have to. He knew what happened because he knew what Keira had done after. She ran.

It was as if everything that had happened the past six years finally all fell into its proper place. The questions were answered, but at what cost?

I think you better go.

Her words still cut through him like a knife. She didn't want him around and who could blame her? He was the very embodiment of everything that had ruined her life. His stepbrother was the one who had stolen her innocence and it was his stepbrother who he had dedicated this entire season to. Everything he'd worked for all wrapped up in a lie.

This whole year, his whole driving force was making up for the guilt of the death of his stepbrother.

It was all a lie.

He grabbed his neck, not knowing what to do or what to think. He needed to get control of his emotions. He sucked in a deep, long breath and then he saw it. Roger's saddle.

It was finished, looking as new as it had when Roger first proudly showed it to Tanner. And Keira had been the one to fix it.

How could she have, after what Roger had done to her?

I asked her, pleaded with her to work on it. How could I?

Tanner stared at it a long moment, his thoughts whirling.

Tomorrow morning he was leaving to compete in the National Finals using this very saddle. Keira had adjusted it so that it fit him better than it had fit Roger.

He had hoped a win would do what the past couple of years of working and praying hadn't been able to. Eradicate the guilt he felt over Roger's death.

Give him deliverance, some way of connecting with Alice and receiving her forgiveness.

His whirling thoughts settled on Alice and the expectations she had heaped on his shoulders moments ago. If he won...

If he made it...

He stared at the saddle, his frustration and fury with his stepbrother growing every minute, a fury that had no outlet because the man he wanted to beat to a pulp for what he had done to the woman he loved was beyond his reach. Roger was already dead. Tanner grabbed the saddle and in one furious heave pitched it against the door of the shop. It landed against the door with a dull thud and then bounced on the floor. Tanner strode over to it, lifted his booted foot and stomped on it. Hard. Then again. And again. He wanted to destroy it.

The symbol of his guilt and loss held other, more ominous meanings.

He took out his fury on the saddle.

Minutes later, sweat was dripping down his forehead and blood seemed to cloud his vision as he gasped for air.

How could you? How could you?

He stared at the now-destroyed saddle, feeling cheated. That was too easy. It wasn't enough. A blind fury still held him in its thrall.

He grabbed the saddle and ran out into the dark to his truck. He tossed the saddle into the box and yanked open the truck door. Jumping in, he twisted the keys in the ignition. He didn't wait for it to warm up. Instead, he slammed it into Reverse, tromped on the accelerator as he spun the truck backward, the exhaust momentarily obscuring his vision. Then he whirled the steering wheel around, slapped the gearshift into first gear and with a roar, tore out of the yard. He needed space to think, to process and clear his head.

He needed to get out onto the open road.

He needed to get rid of Roger's saddle. Take it as far away from Keira and Refuge Ranch as he could.

KEIRA STOOD by the window of her bedroom, watching the blink of Tanner's taillights as his truck sped out of the yard and down the driveway.

She rocked back and forth a moment, trying to find a center of peace and control.

But it eluded her.

I shouldn't have told him.

The insidious words wound themselves around her like a serpent.

If I had kept it to myself, he would still be here.

But she knew that sooner or later the secret would make

itself known. And the longer she kept it to herself, the more harmful and dangerous the fallout would have been.

I should have told him sooner.

Keira dismissed that thought, as well. She hadn't been ready to tell him now; what would it have been like to tell him earlier?

Hugging herself against an all-pervasive chill, she turned away from the window and trudged to her bed. She should go downstairs and help Alice and her mother. And what? Tell them what happened? Talk to Alice, the woman who had almost made her want to explode when she said that Tanner would never be the man Roger was? Explain that because of the evil her son had done to her, Tanner had left in such a rush?

A band of pain constricted her heart.

Tanner.

The look of shocked horror on his face jolted into her mind, and her legs gave way under her. She dropped onto her bed and pressed her hot, tear-streaked face into her hands.

She'd thought she was done crying over what Roger had done. Those years in Edmonton when she was floundering, trying to find her way past the horror and the shame of an event that sundered her life, she thought she had wrung every possible tear out of her eyes.

But here they were again. Only this time it wasn't Roger's actions that caused her sorrow. It was the result of them. Her changing feelings for Tanner had made her vulnerable again. Had created this turmoil of emotions and pain and loss.

Tanner was gone.

She pressed the heels of her hands against her hot eyes, willing the anger and the humiliation away. She waited a moment, trying to still her heart, slow her thoughts.

Nothing has changed from two weeks ago, she reminded herself. You're in the same place.

But she wasn't the same person. She had tasted the sweetness of a reunion with the only man she had ever loved. She'd experienced hope, had dared to look into the future. Her life had expanded and blossomed. Tanner filled a hole in her life that had been empty since she left him.

She couldn't go back.

She tugged a few tissues out of the box beside her bed, wiped her eyes and hands. Then she picked up her Bible and turned back to the passage she had bookmarked with an old letter Tanner had given her years ago. His version of a valentine. Isaiah 43.

"When you pass through the waters, I will be with you; and when you pass through the rivers, they will not sweep over you."

She clung to the words, letting God's strength and love seep into her soul. The waters had swept over her and had sent her running to Edmonton. She'd found a job and had turned her back on God. But He had not turned His back on her. A regular customer at the diner where she worked convinced Keira to come to her church. It was there she met a woman who was a crisis counselor, who seemed to recognize the unspoken pain and guilt in Keira's life. She'd persuaded Keira to see her for counseling. It was in her office, with her prayers and support, that Keira had received strength. When she'd heard that Roger died, she'd been ready to come back. Dana, the counselor, had encouraged Keira to talk to her parents and tell them what happened.

But when Keira came back to Refuge Ranch, she found she couldn't. They were so happy to see her. They'd already had so much trouble with Lee and Heather that she didn't dare add to their burden.

So she'd kept it to herself.

Now Tanner knew and look how that turned out.

Yet, despite that, she felt a certain lightness to her soul. The secret was out, and despite the painful consequences, for the first time in years she felt as if a burden had shifted off her shoulders. For better or worse, someone else carried it now.

And after telling Tanner, she knew it would be easier to tell her parents.

Keira turned the page in the Bible, her eyes resting on the words that had given her strength repeatedly. "Forget the former things; do not dwell on the past." *See, I am doing a new thing!*

She looked straight ahead, letting herself rest in the comfort of those words. She had to look ahead.

Her heart stuttered and her throat thickened. Ahead? To what?

But she caught herself. God was her refuge and strength. He had swept away her sins like a morning mist. He had redeemed her.

She had to remember that no matter what other people thought, God knew her name. God knew her heart. God loved her exactly as she was right now. It didn't matter where she was or whom she was with. She would always have God's love and forgiveness.

Help me to keep my thoughts on You, Lord, she prayed, pressing her fingers against eyes aching from crying. *Help me to trust in You and to know that Your love is perfect and complete. Help me to know that in You is peace and rest no matter where I am.*

Unbidden, her thoughts went to Alice. Roger. Tanner's father. She had harbored so much anger against all of them and it had defined her life the past few years.

She needed to forget the former things in more ways than one, she realized with a start. But could she? And how?

Help me to forgive.

She waited a moment, as if to let that last prayer solidify. She had come back to Refuge Ranch only when she found out that Roger was gone. Only then did she feel safe. But at the same time, despite being home, she still felt as if something was missing in her life.

Then Tanner had come back, and she realized how much he still meant to her.

She felt a jolt of sorrow and then, on its heels, the reminder that God's love was constant and ever present.

With that in mind she got up and went down the stairs to her parents and their questions.

The first person she saw was Alice. She had a tea tray and was carrying it from the kitchen into the living room. She looked up when she saw Keira and her expression hardened. "How are you feeling?" she asked, her voice holding a sting that created a mixture of sorrow and anger in Keira.

But she ignored Alice and continued walking down the stairs. Her parents, sitting in their chairs flanking the fireplace, looked up when she came in, their expressions full of concern blended with curiosity.

What do I tell them? What do I say?

She clung to the moment of peace she had felt only a few moments ago and, knowing that her parents loved her, she sat herself down beside her mother.

"So, you know we're going to ask what's happening," her mother said, her voice strained from a combination of stress, Keira presumed, and from the weariness that usually hit her this time of the day.

"Where's Tanner?" Alice asked.

"He's gone. I don't know where he is."

"Did you try to text him? Is he leaving for Vegas?" Her words were like sharp stabs and Keira wound her hands around each other, holding in her frustration.

Help me to forgive her, Lord, she prayed. She probably doesn't know what happened.

"Alice, I think we should let Keira say what she wants or needs to say," Monty said quietly, but firmly. "In fact, do you want to be alone with us?" Monty continued, turning to Keira, his gentle loving tone pushing at her resolve.

Keira knew what she had to say would tear apart the foundations of Alice's world, as well. And while she didn't care for Alice that much, she couldn't do that to her.

"I think it would be best," she said.

Alice huffed a moment, but then got up. "I'll be in my bedroom," she said, her face pinched with disapproval. Then she left, her footsteps echoing down the hallway leading to the bedroom across from her parents'.

Keira waited to hear the door shut behind her, then eased out a sigh, her hands still clasped tightly together.

"This is really hard," she said, forcing herself to speak quietly. Calmly. "It has to do with why Tanner left. And you also need to know. I'm scared." She took a deep breath, getting herself centered, ready. Then she felt her mother's hand cover hers.

"You never have to be afraid to tell us anything. You are our daughter, and we love you. Unconditionally."

Her mother's voice was warm with love and caring, but Keira also caught a thread of fear. As if her mother had hoped that surely, one of their three children could have come this far unscathed by life's disappointments.

"I know that. And you need to know that I'm...I'm...sorry." She sent up another quick prayer and then she told them everything she had told Tanner. And more.

CHAPTER FOURTEEN

Tanner knew he shouldn't be driving. It was late and he was tired.

But what else could he do? He couldn't go back to the ranch and face Keira. Not after what she'd told him. Not after he'd been going on and on about how he was going to dedicate this season to his stepbrother.

No wonder she wanted him gone.

He stared at his headlights illuminating the darkened road. Vegas was still a twelve-hour drive away. He wouldn't get there tonight.

But once he hit the open road, he couldn't stop. He needed to clear his head, to find a place in his mind for what Keira had told him. To figure out if he still had a place in her life.

She didn't want him around and he didn't blame her. He didn't deserve to be around her, either.

His thoughts jumped back and forth between the year he'd just spent seeking a way to make peace with the guilt that drove him so hard. Guilt over the death of a man he didn't know anymore.

Roger had been his stepbrother.

And he'd done this horrible thing to the woman he loved.

How was he supposed to carry on? And yet, what else could he do? He felt as if the events of the past year inexorably drew him on to Vegas. The end of his long journey.

The original plan had been for him to leave tomorrow anyhow, headed down a journey that was the culmination of a year's work. He'd made so many sacrifices to do this. His health, his business, any kind of personal life—all pushed aside and neglected for this one goal.

The memory of Roger had been with him every time he'd strapped Roger's saddle on the heaving sides of a bronc. Every time he climbed on and got himself ready. Every time he got hurt and got up and rode again.

Every win that took him closer to absolving him of the guilt that haunted him from the moment he'd gotten that phone call.

And then Alice, telling him that the future of the ranch also hung on an eight-second ride.

What was he going to do about that?

Trouble was, he knew he couldn't go back, not after what Keira had said.

Why should she want him around, a daily reminder of what had happened?

But another part of him knew that wasn't entirely true. They'd had some wonderful times together the past few days. Each moment he was with her, he felt as if he had come back to where he belonged.

But how could he face her when the main reason he'd come to her ranch was for her father to fix the saddle of the man who had hurt her so badly. All so he could finish a year dedicated to that same man.

For now, he had no other place to go and nothing else to do so he kept driving and, when he hit the interstate, he turned his truck toward the road that would take him to Vegas.

"Hey, Sugar, what do you think? Felt good to get out, didn't it?" Keira petted her dog on the head, then unwound the scarf she'd had wrapped around her neck and head.

After telling her parents about Roger the other night, they had prayed together, cried together, then Keira had retreated to her bedroom. After a fitful night, she awoke as soon as the sun was up and went for a drive. She knew her parents were worried about her, but she needed some time alone. When she came back, they said nothing. But she sensed their concern in the gentle looks they gave her. Alice was, thankfully, quiet.

This morning she went for a walk, then, instead of going to the house, went directly to the shop hoping to lose herself in her work.

She hung up her scarf and coat, shivering as she walked over to the furnace to turn it up. As she did, her foot scuffed a piece of metal that clanged off the base of the workbench. Puzzled, she picked it up and her heart dropped.

A D ring from a saddle. The only saddle she'd been working on the past while was Roger's.

She closed her eyes, took in a few long, slow breaths to still her roiling emotions.

You are all I need, Lord. You know who I am. You know my name.

She tossed the ring in the garbage. It made a ting on the metal and Sugar walked over as if to investigate. She gave a short whuff, trotted back to her dog bed and dropped onto it, head resting on her paws.

"Yeah, that's the last we'll see of Roger's saddle," Keira said to her dog as she walked around the workbench to the stack of leather.

She squeezed her fists, trying not to think of Tanner. She knew he was probably already in Vegas and why would that change? He had a job to do, a mission to accomplish. Besides, she had been the one who had told him to leave.

Again, she pushed the thoughts aside and started working. The monotony of laying out and cutting the same patterns again and again, the snick of the scissors through the thick leather and then, the steady tempo of the sewing machine as she worked created a rhythm that banked the worst of her pain.

She knew it would come back, but for now her work kept her mind busy enough to reduce Tanner to a shadow in the background.

She worked all through lunch, ignoring the rumblings of her stomach; thankful her father had left her alone for now.

But then, later in the afternoon, the door of the shop creaked open, and Sugar let out a welcoming bark.

Keira couldn't help it. Her heart jumped with hope, and she spun around. But it was only her father stepping inside.

"Hey, you. Guessed you wanted to be left alone for awhile, but I needed to see how you're doing." He kept his distance, as if waiting to see what she needed.

Keira tamped down her foolish reaction, and the unwelcome disappointment that followed it. "I'm trying to catch up in time for the next show. Thanks for asking." She gave him a tight smile. "I know this was hard news for you. Sorry I didn't want to be around yesterday."

"I figured you needed some time alone." He gave her a tender smile. "I am so sorry...my heart. It breaks. I can't imagine how you are dealing with this."

"I've been living with it for the past five years, Dad."

"I know, but still..." He let the sentence drift off as he came closer then stopped by the workbench, restacking some of the leather pieces that had slipped off the pile. He cleared his throat and Keira steeled herself for whatever it was he had to tell her.

"You need to tell Alice," Monty said.

"Tell her what part of the story and how?" Keira snipped an errant thread and set the piece she'd been working on aside.

Monty sighed. "I'm not sure. But I believe she needs to know. Not to show her what a snake Roger was, but to let her see that she's been wrong to treat Tanner as she has."

"Do you think telling her what Roger did to me will change that?"

Monty sighed. "I don't know. I just feel so strongly about what has happened to Tanner. I want to make it right. Everyone in the valley knows it wasn't right for Tanner to be treated the way he was."

Keira looked down at her hands, absently pushing back a cuticle as she considered what her father told her. "She might not believe me," Keira said, stating the other possibility. "And I can't face that."

"I understand, honey. But I do believe parents know, in their hearts, when their kids did right and when they did wrong."

"Do you believe Lee ran over Abby Newton's father? Do you believe he did what he was accused of?"

Her father's gaze narrowed and for a moment Keira felt she had overstepped her boundaries. "He was in the driver's seat of his truck when the sheriff found him. He was tried by a judge and found guilty," was her father's evasive reply.

Keira looked away. "Well, I don't believe he did it, regardless of what Cornell Newton said he saw. Why would Alice think any different if I told her what Roger did? It would be my word against the memory of a son she spoiled and idealized. No eyewitnesses at all."

The only sound in the silence that followed her words was the deep breathing of Sugar, oblivious to the upheavals in the lives of her masters.

"Another thing, I know I'm supposed to be forgiving," Keira continued. "I want to forgive her and…Roger. But it's so hard. I know that lack of forgiveness had kept me away from church for a while and I don't want what happened to me to define my life. If I can't forgive her or Roger, I feel like what happened will always be attached to me. Like a barnacle I can't get rid of."

Her father walked over to her, knelt beside her and gave her a quick, hard hug. "Don't carry that weight so hard, my dear. God knows how you are feeling about this. He understands your pain and He knows how hard it can be to forgive. This is a huge thing you've had to deal with. Forgiving this is going to take time and that's good. To forgive too quickly is to skip over the process of healing you need to go through and to minimize this horrible thing that happened."

Keira rested her head against her father's shoulder. "Thanks, Daddy," she whispered. "How did you get to be so wise?"

"Not so wise, honey," he said, and Keira heard the regret in his voice. "If I was wise, I would have seen what was going on. I might have intervened when you and Tanner were fighting, made room on the ranch for you both. I guessed I had kept hoping Alice would do the right thing." Then Monty pushed himself to his feet. "Which is why Alice needs to know."

"Maybe, but even if I tell her and she agrees to do the right thing, what difference will that make?" she asked, suddenly weary and wrung out. "Tanner's gone. I doubt he's coming back."

"Don't ever underestimate that man," he said quietly. "He'll do what's right."

Monty laid his hand on her shoulder. She looked up at him, catching the sorrow in his eyes. "I always said I didn't want to be the kind of person who was blind to his children's faults. Heather and Lee haven't made good choices. Lee was living a life that didn't honor God or us, and Heather always went her own way. Maybe you made a couple of bad choices, too, but you, of all my children, did not deserve to have this horrible—" his hand tightened on her shoulder a minute, then released "—

horrible thing happen to you. And if it was my son who did it, I would want to know."

Keira's only response was a tight nod.

"We're going to eat supper in a few minutes, then we're watching the National Finals. Just thought I would warn you."

"Thanks," was all she said. "I'll see how I feel."

Monty patted her once more on the shoulder, then left.

Keira sat a moment, staring into space, her heart aching. She didn't want to watch Tanner compete but at the same time, part of her wanted to have a different picture in her mind than of the anger in his face.

She wanted to see him smile.

Wanted one good memory to tuck away for the time ahead.

CHAPTER FIFTEEN

"*L*et's leave the dishes until after," Ellen said as she looked at the clock on the wall behind Keira. Dinner was over and Keira got up to start clearing. "The Finals are about to start."

"You watch." Keira shooed her parents and Alice away. "I'll take care of this."

Her father, never the most eager dishwasher, gave her a grin of thanks and scurried off to the living room.

"But aren't you coming?" her mother asked, as she slowly got to her feet.

"It won't take long," Keira assured her. "I'll join you when I'm done."

Her mother gave her an understanding smile and followed Alice into the living room.

Keira took her time stacking plates and rinsing them, torn between the need to protect her heart and the desire to see Tanner one more time.

Pain stabbed her chest and she faltered, thinking of the emptiness that yawned ahead of her. Then she caught herself and straightened.

Please help me through this, Lord, she prayed. Help me get through this hard, harrowing pain. Help me to know that You are my all in all.

She was finally finishing up when she heard Alice call out, "Keira, it's starting."

Does she have any idea of what she's doing to me? Keira thought, snapping the tea towel she had dried the pots with. She fought down her anger but then, when she heard the music starting up and announcers talking, she walked over to the entrance of the living room and stood in the doorway.

On the television hanging on the wall at right angles to her parents' chairs she saw two smiling announcers in cowboy hats and Western shirts superimposed over the yawning arena behind them, packed with spectators. They were talking about the opening of the NFR, who was headlining the venues, the many sponsors of this show—all just talk to fill up space until the opening ceremonies.

Keira leaned against the doorway, her heart hurrying as she felt the anticipation building. She used to watch Tanner compete whenever she could and each time, she'd felt this same sense of dread mingled with nervous excitement.

The announcers thanked the sponsors again and talked for a while about the history of the NFR. Keira was about to leave when, behind them, she saw the competitors entering the ring in preparation for the opening ceremonies. There were so many competitors, she thought as she leaned forward trying to see if she could catch Tanner, his gray hat pulled low over his face. But the cowboys and cowgirls on horseback behind the announcers were too small to see as they lined up.

"Surprising news tonight coming from the saddle bronc field of competitors," the announcer was saying. Keira's heart flipped again. "It's been a tight race all year but for a while it looked like Brad Butler had first place locked up coming into this competition. Now, Brad as you know, broke his ankle," the one announcer said, frowning at the other. "So that put Zeke Redenbauch and Tanner Fortier in tight competition for first place. But this afternoon we got some huge news."

"Yes, Dick, apparently we've had a major upset today in the field," the other announcer said, looking directly at the camera. "One of the heavily favored contenders, Tanner Fortier, has bowed out of the competition."

"What?"

"No."

Monty and Alice called out at the same time.

Keira could only stare at the television, the mouths of the announcers still moving as she tried to absorb what they were saying.

Tanner? Dropped out of the competition?

"We had heard that he was on some type of quest this year in honor of his stepbrother, Roger, who, as you know, died tragically two years ago," Dick was saying, "We had hoped to talk to Tanner about it, but he wasn't available for an interview earlier and then, an hour later we got the official announcement."

The other announcer shook his head in surprise. "Apparently it had nothing to do with an injury. The only information we got was that he told a fellow competitor last night he couldn't finish this. That he had something more important to do."

"Cryptic comments from a cryptic cowboy," the other announcer said. "Tanner's the kind of guy who plays his cards close to his chest. So, we might never find out why he ducked out now when this title was practically his for the taking." Then the announcer paused, looking back over his shoulder. "And it looks like we're getting ready for the opening—"

"What is Tanner thinking?" Alice proclaimed. "How could he do this?"

Keira didn't know what to think.

Then a knock on the door just off the kitchen behind her

gave her a start. She walked to the porch, still trying to absorb what had happened.

She opened the door. And her heart stopped.

Tanner stood outside, his hat in his hand, his eyes clinging to hers.

"I couldn't do it," was all he said.

KEIRA WAS STARING AT HIM, a dish towel slung over her shoulder, her eyes wide, her mouth hanging open, her hair pulled back in an untidy ponytail.

Looking even more beautiful than he had ever imagined. His heart thudded in his chest and the prayers that he had sent up all the way here coalesced into this moment. *Please, Lord, let her take me back.*

"What are you doing here? What... How...?" she stammered, twisting the dish towel in her hands.

"Can I come in?" He wasn't sure how to handle her, what to say. He felt as if he had to be so careful with her and yet, she held his eyes, her gaze steady.

"Of course." She stood aside and he stepped inside the porch, pulling his boots off, shrugging off his coat. The porch was warm compared to the chill of his truck and he shivered a moment as he pulled his hat off.

"Why are you here? We were just watching the opening ceremonies. They said you left."

"I couldn't compete," he said quietly, keeping his eyes fixed on hers, praying, hoping she would hear him out. "After what you told me about Roger, it didn't matter anymore. I couldn't do that to you, so I left."

He didn't know if it was his wayward, hungry heart that caught a look of yearning in her expression. But the fact that she hadn't moved away from him, the fact that her eyes seemed to cling to his, gave him the encouragement to move close enough that the scent of her perfume teased his nostrils. His heart plunged and he had to fight his own hunger to pull her into his arms.

"But what about your plan to dedicate this year to Roger?"

"Roger had no right to have anything done in his memory."

Her lips trembled and he saw moisture welling up in her eyes. "You gave up your whole year? All the work before that?"

He just shook his head, her sorrow unmanning him. Again, anger gripped his soul and again he had to push it down. He didn't want her to be afraid of him.

"The competition, the past year, all meant nothing. If I couldn't have you with me, then I didn't want to have anything else." He drew in a long, slow breath, encouraged by the fact that she hadn't stepped away from him. That she was still looking at him. "I know you told me to leave, and I tried," he said, keeping his voice quiet, like he would with a scared filly. "But I can't stay away from you. I'm hoping, with time, we can get through this. I don't want to give up on us. I love you."

"Tanner," she breathed, her hands lifting toward him. "I don't want to give up on us, either."

Her words were like a drink of water to a man dying of thirst. He took a quick step, closing the distance between them. He wrapped one arm around her and nudged her chin up with his knuckle. Her eyes sparkled with tears, and one slowly tracked down her cheek. He thumbed it away. "I want to kiss you," he said quietly. He wasn't sure how to deal with her. He felt as if he had to be careful, cautious.

"You don't need to ask," she said, rising to meet him.

Their lips met, melded, and Tanner felt as if all the broken places of his life had finally become whole.

He slowly drew back again. "I love you," was all he could say. "I've always loved you."

Keira blinked and another tear escaped. "I don't think I've ever stopped loving you. I missed you so much."

"Oh, Keira, the years we've lost." He had to fight another surge of anger at his stepbrother and what he had done to both of them. "Roger... I can't begin to say... I'm so sorry."

She stopped him with another kiss. "It wasn't your fault."

"And my father and Alice. I'm trying so hard not to be angry with them." He drew in a sharp breath. "I wish I had known. I wish you had told me." Then he stopped there, realizing he was putting yet another burden on her shoulders. "I wished I could have helped you."

She touched his lips, her smile holding a note of melancholy. "I should have trusted that you wanted to take care of me. I was just so ashamed. So scared of what you might think."

Tanner sighed, cradling his face in hers. "What you should have been scared of is what I would have done to Roger had I known."

She pressed a finger to his lips. "I don't want to talk about Roger anymore."

"I know. I just wished I would have paid more attention to you. Listened more."

"You're not the only one," she said. "We should have talked more and fought less. Stopped, each of us, trying to impose our will on the other. I should have been willing to give up being here to be with you. I know I've spent enough time being angry. I know that it's taken up too much of my past. I don't want it to be part of our future." She drew away, her finger trailing down his face and resting on a button of his shirt. "I know I've always said I would never leave Aspen Valley, but I missed you so much." Then, to his surprise, she added, "And if it means that I must leave Refuge Ranch so that we can be together, then so be it. I'd sooner be in Lethbridge with you than in Aspen Valley alone."

Tanner could only stare, knowing what those words cost

CAROLYNE AARSEN

her. He wanted to assure her that wouldn't be the case, but he knew he couldn't.

"We'll see what the future brings," he said. "I wish I could promise you all the things I want to—"

She stopped him. "I do, too. But I don't want to be apart again. It hurts too much."

He kissed her again, wishing, praying, they could find a way through this.

"I want to help you. I want to be here for you," was all he could say.

"You're here now and that's all that matters."

"Who you talking to?" Monty called from the living room, thundering into the moment. "Who came to the door?"

"Here we go," Tanner breathed.

"I guess we'll have to face them sooner or later," Keira said, giving him another kiss.

Then he took her hand and leading the way, walked back through the kitchen to the living room.

The first thing Tanner saw was the back of Alice's head leaning forward, facing the television. Ellen and Monty sat in their chairs, staring at the screen. He heard the thunder of the music as lights flashed. All part of the opening ceremonies.

"We were just watching...the program..." Keira stopped, clinging to his hand.

"Bring whoever is out there in here," Monty called out, a touch of asperity in his voice, eyes glued to the television.

Though Tanner had foolishly hoped he might catch Keira on her own, he knew if he came to the house, he would have to face everyone all at once.

May as well get it over and done with. Time with Keira would have to wait.

"It's Tanner," Keira announced.

Monty looked over, puzzled, then surged to his feet, staring.

"Tanner Fortier, what in the world are you doing here?" he boomed.

Alice spun around on the couch, her mouth a perfect O of shock. She looked from the screen back to Tanner, then to the television again as if she hoped, by some trick of technology, he would still show up on the screen and compete.

"I'm sorry, Alice," he said to his stepmother, needing to get that out of the way. "I couldn't compete. Not knowing what Roger did."

"Tanner," Keira whispered from behind. "She doesn't know."

Tanner spun around. "You didn't tell her?"

"I couldn't. Not yet."

He wanted to ask her more, but then Monty was at his side, hand on his shoulder. "You didn't go through with it? All your hard work—"

"It's over," Tanner said quietly.

"Why aren't you competing? Why aren't you there?" Alice's voice took on a shrill tone as she came around the couch. "After what you said... Why did you quit? Doesn't Roger mean anything to you?"

Tanner straightened and held Alice's glare. "No. He doesn't."

"How can you say such a thing?"

To Tanner's surprise, he thought she would be angrier, but as she looked at him, he caught a glimpse of sorrow. As if, on some level, she knew.

"I think we should discuss this in the study," Monty said.

"No, this is between me and my son," Alice said quietly, but Tanner heard the thread of steel in her voice.

"Actually, all of us here are affected," Tanner said. "Though I don't know if Ellen needs to be involved." He was sure, from the way she was looking from Keira to Alice, that she knew what had happened. He just didn't want her to witness any drama that might ensue.

"I'm fine," Ellen protested. "I'm not some orchid that needs pampering. Sit down here if you need to talk things out. I know what's been happening."

Alice was still looking at him, as if she didn't know what to make of him.

Tanner wasn't sure what to think, but with Keira at his side, still holding his hand, he found it didn't matter anymore what Alice thought.

"Okay, then, let's sit down."

Monty led the way and Tanner, still holding Keira's hand, walked over to the love seat. He glanced at Keira and squeezed her hand. Whatever happened now, come what may, at least he and Keira were together. They could face this, together.

CHAPTER SIXTEEN

*K*eira clung to his hand as Tanner eased himself down on the love seat. She couldn't keep her eyes off him. Couldn't believe he had done this. She knew how hard he had worked and how much he had sacrificed to make this final run to the NFR.

But now, instead of being saddled to the back of a snorting bronco, riding for his stepbrother, he was here. He had thrown everything away to be with her.

Tanner squeezed her hand harder, his eyes still on her, then he turned back to the gathering.

"First off, before I say anything more, I want everyone here, Monty and Ellen especially, to know that I love Keira," he said, his voice ringing with a conviction that created a quieting in her chest. "I don't want to be apart from her anymore and I'm hoping she feels the same way about me. I know we were engaged before, but this time around I feel like we both know what we want and how to keep it."

"I know I do," Keira said, returning his smile and despite the audience, kissing him gently, as if to seal her promise.

Tanner turned back to Alice.

"But now, there's something I need to discuss with you that concerns my and Keira's future. I haven't talked to you much about Dad's will. I was afraid to face you. Afraid of finding out how you really felt about me, finding out how my father felt about me, so I avoided it." He looked back at Keira and gave her another quick hug. "But I learned a lesson in facing fears from a very strong person."

His words settled into her soul and for the first time in years she felt the shame of what had happened lose its strength.

"At one time I hired a lawyer to contest the will," Tanner continued, talking to Alice. "But after Roger's death, I couldn't do that to you. So, I dropped the suit. However, the ranch belonged to my father. That nothing of it came to me isn't right."

Alice held his gaze a moment as if challenging him. "Your father owed me," she said quietly.

"What do you mean?"

Alice's eyes ticked from Tanner to Keira as if she was still unhappy with the situation, but Keira simply held her gaze, refusing to back down. Tanner thought she was strong. Well, she could be strong with him beside her.

Alice wound her hands around each other, her eyes fixed on her twisting fingers. "Your father and I got married in Regina," she said, her voice quiet as she moved to the past. "We met on a previous trip he made there to look at some cattle. The reason he came back the second time was because I was pregnant. I told him he had to do something about it, so he married me. He wanted to do right by me, and he wanted someone to take care of you."

Tanner's quick intake of breath and the look of surprise on her parents' faces told Keira that this was truly all news to them. "Very few people know this," Alice continued, "but that was why we got married. I know we fought a lot, but before he died, we had come to a kind of peace. And when he died, he willed the ranch to me with the idea that I would share it equally between you and Roger."

Keira could only stare at Alice, growing even angrier with the woman. Her decision and subsequent favoring of Roger had had huge, long-lasting repercussions for her and Tanner. But it wasn't her place to say anything. Instead, she could only cling to Tanner, offering him the support she could.

"If that's true, why did you make it so clear that Roger was the one to get the ranch? Not me?"

"Like I said, I felt like your father owed me," Alice continued, but she couldn't look at either Keira or Tanner. "I didn't want to live out here, but I had no choice. I hated every moment of it. And you weren't his natural son."

"But you're still here," Keira couldn't help but mention.

"I stayed because of Roger. I thought if something could come of this for Roger, then it would be worth it."

"And where did I fit into your life?" Tanner's voice held an edge of steely resolve. As if he needed to get this out of the way.

"I came to care for you, too," she said. Then she looked over at Ellen, as if hoping she would intervene for her. "I wasn't a bad mother. And as I got to know you and Monty, I started to think maybe I could stay here. You've both been such a help to me when Cyrus died and then when Roger died."

"Of course," Ellen said. "That's what friends do."

"We care for you as a friend," Monty was saying. "But I can't stay quiet about this any longer. I have to say we never understood how you could favor Roger over Tanner. You know, in your heart, that this isn't right. Tanner shouldn't have to earn what his father had entrusted you to give to him. I have been quiet about this, and I was wrong to not say anything before. But if you examine your heart, you'll know that I'm right. You need to give Tanner half of the ranch, as Cyrus would have wanted it."

Silence followed that proclamation and Keira felt a knock of pride against her ribs. Her father could speak with such quiet authority. How could Alice not pay attention?

"Roger was my son," Alice said. "Cyrus's only true son. And he wanted so badly to ranch."

"Tanner was your son, too," Ellen said quietly. "And Tanner was a good son."

But then Ellen glanced at Keira as if acknowledging the difference between Tanner and his stepbrother. She gave her a careful smile, and, in that smile, Keira recognized that whatever she decided to say or not say, her mother and father would stand behind her.

Alice released a careful sigh. "So, what do you think I should do?" looking back at Keira and Tanner.

"I know I have always been just a stepson to you," Tanner said. "But I know that in God's eyes I am valuable and I'm His son as much as any other person. I don't need to have your blessing, but I want to appeal to your sense of honor. If you think I should buy you out, I will find a way to do that. If you want to do it differently, then we can discuss that. But I am not leaving anymore." He glanced over at Keira, his eyes holding her. "I know that I belong here, with Keira, in the valley, and I'll find a way to make that happen."

Her heart thrilled at the intensity in his voice, at the conviction in his words.

"But you were going to compete for Roger," Alice pressed. "What about him? What about his memory? Doesn't that mean anything to you?" Then Alice turned to Keira. "Did you talk him out of this? Was this because of you?"

Keira heard her father's gasp, fought down her own surge of pain and anger as she felt Tanner's hand tighten on hers, knowing that while her own emotions had to be kept out of it, Alice needed to keep the focus on the future. Not the past.

"Tanner made the right decision," she said, facing Alice head-on. "While I'm sad for his sake he didn't compete, I'm glad he didn't do it and, like he said, someday we'll explain why. But I had nothing to do with why he came back. That was his own call. And I'm glad he did. I know you loved Roger, but the sacrifices Tanner made for Roger were for the wrong reason and the wrong person."

Alice looked baffled, as if trying to catch up to what Keira was saying.

"You also need to know that Roger and I never really dated," Keira continued. "We went to a couple of parties together. I never, ever, had any intention of marrying him. He wasn't the man Tanner is and he never could be."

"But he told me that he loved you." Alice's voice held a note of pleading, as if she couldn't understand why Keira would choose Tanner over Roger.

Keira felt the old chill entering her soul. The old shame. Yet as they slipped up past her defenses, she felt the warmth of Tanner's body beside her, the support of his arm slipping around her shoulders, pulling her even closer.

She couldn't let this take over. She couldn't let Roger dominate her life anymore.

And then, in a flash of insight, as she held Alice's intent gaze, she had an inspiration.

"I know how Roger felt about Tanner. He looked up to him so much and idealized him. Remember how, when he was little, he used to wear Tanner's boots? His shirt? How he would pretend to be Tanner?" Keira leaned forward, pushing down her own emotions, praying for something she was saying to connect with Alice. She knew Alice thirsted for stories of Roger and though Keira's most current stories were not ones to share, she had others that she could. And in sharing those stories, Keira felt that she was, at the same time, loosening the stranglehold Roger's assault on her held on her memories.

"I forgot about that," Alice said, a faint smile easing away the harshness that had tightened her features.

"He loved Tanner," Keira said. "When he was five, didn't he put some dirt in his hair because he wanted it to be dark? Like Tanner's?"

"Remember that time I found that frog for him?" Tanner said, playing along.

"He put it in a jar and carried it everywhere." Keira's laugh, this time, was more genuine as she hearkened back to happier, less complicated times.

Alice laughed, as well. "He did love that frog. I think he even called him Tanner."

They all chuckled together a moment and, in the background, Keira caught her parents' puzzled looks. As if they couldn't understand what Keira was doing with the memories of a man who had done such a horrible thing to her.

But she ignored them and pressed on, a new determination entering her soul.

"We know Roger loved Tanner," she said, turning back to Alice. "He worshipped him. And I don't think, despite all the things that happened, that Roger stopped loving his older brother. And I think that Roger would want you to do the right thing with the ranch. With the brother he loved so much."

Alice drew back a moment; as if suddenly unsure of the direction Keira had taken her and yet, even as wariness clouded her features, Keira could see she had struck a chord. "Maybe," she said, still prevaricating. Still holding out.

But Keira held her gaze, determined to put recent memories aside for Tanner's sake. "I'm not asking for me. I'm asking for Tanner. He's the only son you've got left regardless of who his father was. Roger would want him to have the ranch. As much as I know about Roger, I know that to be true."

She held Alice's puzzled gaze, felt Tanner's arm around her, and in that moment, she felt as if Roger's grip on her memories had lost some of their strength.

Then Alice blinked and Keira saw a track of moisture trickle down her cheek. "You know, I think you may be right." Then she gave Tanner a wan smile. "I'm sorry I didn't talk to you sooner about this. I guess I still was clinging to my memories of Roger and was too wrapped up in my own loss. Will you forgive me?"

The question hovered and Keira knew, for a fact, that someday they would have to tell her about Roger.

But not yet.

"Of course, I forgive you," Tanner said, getting to his feet and bending over to give Alice a quick hug. "You're the only mother I have."

She sniffed and nodded. "Thank you for that. And I know what I must do. With the ranch. It was your father's, after all."

"But we can talk about this more later." Tanner turned to Keira and held out his hand. Keira put hers in it as he gently pulled her to her feet. "As for you and me, we have other things to discuss."

Keira's heart thrilled with the promise in his voice and the love in his eyes.

Then she followed him out of the room and to the porch, where they threw on some coats, boots and hurried out to the shop.

TANNER SET himself down on the old office chair that was tucked up against the desk in the workshop. Then, with a smile, he pulled Keira onto his lap and eased out a long, satisfied sigh as he wrapped his arms around her.

"So, this is where my latest adventure started," Tanner said, holding Keira close, tucking her head under his chin. "I think it only appropriate that this is where I hope to put a happy ending to this part of our story."

Keira chuckled, her throaty voice thrilling his soul. Then, after a few moments of silence, she traced gentle circles on the button of his pocket. "Do you think Alice will really give you the ranch?"

"I think she will. I think what you said made a difference." He held her closer, if that was even possible. "I can't believe you were able to pull out those old memories. I thought even saying his name would be difficult for you."

Keira heard the faint thumping of Tanner's heart below her ear, a steady solid rhythm. Just like the man who held her, and his arms felt like home.

"I don't want Roger to have any hold over me, and bringing up those memories reminded me that, at one time, he was just a cute, fun kid who loved and looked up to you."

Tanner felt a surge of admiration for this amazing woman who lay in his arms, a miracle in so many ways.

Then, ignoring her protests, he straightened, setting her upright. "But let's not dwell on the former things," he said, appropriating the text she'd underlined in her Bible. "I have something important to do right now," he said quietly, unbuttoning the pocket of his shirt.

He dug around then carefully pulled out the engagement ring he had once given Keira. As it sparkled in the light, he heard Keira's indrawn gasp of surprise.

"You still have it," she breathed, one hand resting on her heart as if to contain it.

He turned it around, letting it catch the light. "Yeah. I couldn't get rid of it. It's been sitting in a box beside my bed since you gave it back to me. I got it when I went back to check on the garage. I took it with me to the NFR. Thought it would inspire me. And it did. It inspired me to make my decisions for you and for me." He took her hand, held it up and then looked into her eyes. "Keira Bannister, once again I'm going to ask you, will you marry me?"

Keira's lips trembled, then she nodded her head as he slipped the ring on her finger. "And once again I'm going to say yes."

She wrapped her arms around his neck, he held her close, and they exchanged a kiss that sealed the promise. She drew back, tracing his features with her fingers, her eyes holding his. "I should never have broken up with you the first time," she said. "I promise, I'll stick with you through everything."

He touched her lips with his finger. "It's okay. I'll try not to give you a reason to break up with me. And so much has changed in our lives."

"We have gone through a lot," Keira said quietly, her hand resting on his chest. "And I know that with God's help, we'll get through whatever will come in our future. And we'll do it together."

"Together. I like the sound of that."

"And if you want me to move to Lethbridge—"

He stopped her with another kiss. "I'll be selling the garage," he said. "I'm moving back here. I'm moving back onto my father's ranch."

"Do you think Alice will do what she says?"

He held that thought a moment, then nodded. "She will. I think she's known for a while she should have done right by me, but I never pushed it. I have the best reason to now."

Keira lowered her head, and they shared another kiss. A kiss that sealed their promises to each other.

WANT to find out more about the Cowboys of Aspen Valley - Read more about Keira's sister Heather who has returned back from New York City...

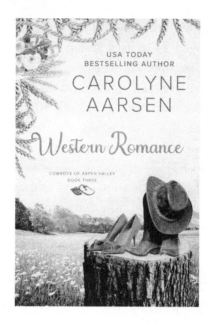

SHE SAW the truck a split second too late.

The sun shining directly in her eyes and the swirling snow of a late spring storm, blinded her as Heather Bannister crested the hill. The pickup was coming right at her and there was nowhere to go.

So she did what any self-respecting country girl would.

She swerved, then stepped on the gas.

The back end of her car fishtailed on the icy patches of gravel as she fought to get it turned away from the truck, praying her tires would grab something. Anything.

She caught a glimpse of a panicked face behind the wheel of the pickup as her tires spun on the road. A split second before she would have been hit, she gained enough traction to shoot her car past the vehicle, missing it by mere inches.

And sending her directly toward the ditch. This time Heather slammed her foot on the brakes and madly turned the steering wheel.

But with a crash and a heavy thud, the side of her car

slammed into the bank of old, spring snow. The impact spun the vehicle around and the front of her vehicle slammed into the icy and packed snow.

Dazed, stunned, and confused, Heather sat a moment, the whine of her car and the ringing in her ears the only sounds she heard.

A heavy ache radiated from her shoulder across her chest and up her neck, surprising in its intensity. For a confused moment Heather wondered if the airbag had even done its job, but it lay, deflated across her lap, proof that it had, in fact, deployed.

Hands still clenched around the steering wheel, Heather sucked in another breath and sent out another cough. Her arms shook and her legs felt suddenly rubbery.

So close.

She had come within inches of a serious accident.

Her heartbeat thundered in her ears as reaction set in. Her legs trembled, adrenaline was replaced by a chill coursing through her body as her mind created images of twisted steel and horrible injuries.

She shook the thoughts off. She couldn't allow herself to think of 'what ifs'. She hadn't hit the truck head on. She had avoided a collision that would have had far worse consequences. She had to cling to that.

As she laid her head back on the headrest, trying to pull herself together, tattered prayers fluttered through her mind.

Thank you, Lord. Forgive me, Lord.

The same feeble petitions she had sent heavenward for the past few years. That was all she'd been capable of in the mess that was her married life with her ex-husband, Mitch.

An insistent banging on her door made her jump, adding to the piercing pain in Heather's head.

Probably the driver of the truck, come to give her an Alberta lecture on road safety and driving to the right when approaching a hill. Things her adoptive father had taught her and her siblings from the time they had turned a key.

"You okay in there?"

The muffled voice outside the car and the continued thumping of a fist on the door made Heather wince again as she painstakingly found the release for the seat belt, then pulled it back over her chest. But when she tried to open the door, it wouldn't budge. Probably got twisted in the crash.

She didn't need this, she thought, allowing herself a moment of self-pity. Stuck in the ditch only five miles from home with a cell phone that was out of juice and some stranger banging on the window.

Then she pulled herself together. City life may have softened her, her ex-husband may have tried to beat her down, but this wasn't her first rodeo. She was an Albertan born and bred and had once been a championship barrel racer. She had been thrown off horses trying to get around a tight barrel, chased by ornery cows, jammed in loading chutes, and raced across rodeo arena's on out-of-control horses. As her father always said, You can take the girl out of the country, but you can't take the country out of the girl.

So she took a deep breath, ignored the pounding in her head, keeping time to the pounding of the man outside, turned in her seat, lifted her booted foot and gave the door a mighty kick.

"Hey, what are you doing?" the man outside the car protested.

"Getting out of here," Heather called back, kicking the door again, wishing she had her sturdy riding boots instead of these flimsy, high-heeled ones. But she managed to create an opening and grabbing her purse, she slithered through it.

Her first step out was onto the icy snow and she would have stumbled forward had not the man outside her car caught her by the arm.

She found her balance then looked up at her would-be rescuer.

And her heart plunged into her stomach.

John Argall.

Son of Russ Argall, Bannister's hired hand and the man she had broken up with to move to New York. One of the people she had most dreaded to face coming back to Refuge Ranch.

His blue eyes, fringed by thick lashes stared down at her, narrowed as if he wasn't sure what he was looking at. "Hello, stranger," he said, but his voice, once warm and friendly was as icy and cold as the snow under her feet.

Not that she blamed him. She was the one who had broken up with him. Who had ignored his warnings about believing Mitch's big plans. She could have saved herself a world of hurt, pain, and regret had she listened to him. Had she not impulsively chased after what she thought would solve her problem.

Just like her mother always did.

"Hello, John," was all she could say, pushing the traitorous thought back. She hadn't returned to Refuge Ranch to indulge in might-have-beens. She was only here to help her mother plan a bridal shower for Keira, even though she wouldn't be able to attend. Then she was off to Seattle to interview for an important job. A step in a new direction. Her debts were finally paid, her obligations fulfilled, and she was ready to start a future on her own, free from any ties and obligations. Free from any romantic entanglements. She had made enough bad decisions in her love life the past few years, she was ready to be free and live on her own.

"So, looks like you're in a bind." He turned back to her car, buried up to its hood in the snowdrift left behind by a late spring snowstorm. "Why don't you go into the truck and warm up while I find a tow rope?"

"I can help," she said lifting her chin, her tone holding a

defiant edge. Anger had been her defense the past years, she deployed it now.

His eyes grazed over her knee-high boots, skirt, and thin wool jacket with its pleats and tiny buttons. She knew the designer clothes were more suited for the runway than Alberta spring weather, but they were the only type of clothes she had after years of living in New York. "You'll just fall in those heels," he said with a deprecating tone that stung. "Besides, I wouldn't mind if you would check on my daughter, Adana. She's in the truck all by herself."

Heather couldn't stop the clench in her stomach as she looked back at John's truck, parked to one side of the road, still running, exhaust wreathing around the cab. Through the fogged up window she saw a car seat and sitting in it, John's little girl, Adana. Through the occasional notes and texts from her family, she had heard about John's marriage to her old friend Samantha, and the birth of his little girl, two years ago, born two days before Samantha died of internal hemorrhaging.

Now the toddler's head bounced back and forth, the bright pink pom-pom on her stocking cap bobbing with each movement as if she was dancing in her seat. She waved mittened hands as she caught John and Heather looking at her.

John's daughter. Samantha's little girl.

Heather swallowed down her apprehension, then gave him a cautious smile, buying herself a few more moments. "By the way, I never had a chance to tell you that I was sorry to hear about Samantha's death. I know it was almost two years ago, but...well...I'm still sorry. It must have been hard for you."

John just looked at her, his expression unchanging. If anything, the set of his jaw seemed grimmer. "Yeah. It was, but like you said, it was awhile ago. We're coping."

His harsh tone cut but she knew she deserved nothing more. She should have written. Should have called. Samantha was a dear friend to Heather as well as John's wife, but Heather had been dealing with her own problems at the time. Still, in spite of Heather's history with John, Heather knew at minimum she owed her childhood friend the courtesy of sending her widower, her old boyfriend, a card.

"I'm sure it's been hard," she said quietly. "Samantha was a good person and at one time, a good friend."

His only reply was a tight nod which made her feel even worse.

So she turned away, taking a careful step, trying to find her footing on melting snow. She faltered, almost losing her balance but then John caught her.

Even through the layers of her coat, she felt the solid grip of his hand on his arm, steadying her.

"I'm okay," she said, surprised at her reaction to his touch. She pulled away, but then almost fell forward, her hands flailing as she struggled to catch her balance.

"Always were too stubborn for your own good," John muttered, catching her again and helping her to the road.

Heather shot him an annoyed glance, but didn't pull away again until she got her feet under her on the road.

"Go warm up," he said, pointing to the truck. "I'll need to attach a tow rope."

Six years ago she would have teased him about being so bossy. But that was when they were dating. When the foolish decisions Heather would make would result in a gentle reprimand from him and a smart remark from her.

Instead, she wrapped her coat around her, ducked her head against the gust of wind that had started up and walked to the truck. She slipped a couple of times on the icy road, unable to get a proper purchase in her high-heeled boots, but she finally made it. As she pulled open the door, happy music, Adana's happy chatter, and blessed heat washed over her in an assault on her senses.

She climbed into the raised truck cab and pulled the door

closed behind her, shivering as she turned to Adana, sitting in her car seat on the passenger side of the truck.

The little girl grew suddenly silent and stared back at her, eyes as blue as John's, curls of blond hair sticking out from her hat.

Adana had John's eyes, his arching eyebrows. But she had her mother's delicate nose and generous smile. Heather gave her a careful smile, an ache, like a rock, settling in her stomach as she looked into eyes that were the same age as her own child would have been.

OTHER SERIES

I have many other books for you to enjoy. Check them out here.

COWBOYS OF ASPEN VALLEY

#1 Western Hearts - December 1, 2021

#2 Western Wishes - January 12, 2022

#3 Western Romance - March 2, 2022

#4 Western Kisses - April 20, 2022

#5 Western Vows - June 8, 2022

#6 Western Blessings - July 20, 2022

ASPEN VALLEY HOMECOMING

#1 The Way Back Home

#2 The Way Back to Faith

#3 The Way Back to Hope

#4 The Way Back to Love

LOVE IN MILLARS CROSSING

#1 A Family's Christmas

#2 A Family's Blessing

#3 A Family's Hope

#4 A Family's Promise

MILLARS CROSSING ROMANCE

#1 COUNTRY ROMANCE

#2 COUNTRY COURTSHIP

#3 COUNTRY PROPOSAL

#4 COUNTRY WEDDING

FAMILY BONDS

#1 SEEKING HOME

A rancher who suffered a tragic loss. A single mother on the edge. Can these two find the courage to face a romantic new beginning?

#2 CHOOSING HOME

If you like emergency room drama, second chances, and quaint small-town settings, then you'll adore this romance.

#3 COMING HOME

He thought she chose a hotel over him. She thought he loved money more than her. Years later, can they fill the emptiness in their hearts?

#4 FINDING HOME

She's hiding a terrible truth. He's trying to overcome his scandalous history. Together, forgiveness might give them a second chance.

FAMILY TIES

Four siblings trying to finding their way back to family and faith

A COWBOY'S REUNION

He's still reeling from the breakup. She's ashamed of what she did. Can a chance reunion mend the fence, or are some hearts forever broken? If you like second chance stories, buried passions, and big country settings, then you'll love this emotional novel.

"I enjoyed this book and had trouble putting it down and had to finish it. If the rest of this series is this great, I look forward to reading more books by Carolyne Aarsen." Karen Semones - Amazon Review

THE COWBOY'S FAMILY

She's desperate. He's loyal. Will a dark lie hold them back from finding love on the ranch? If you like determined heroines, charming cowboys, and family dramas, then you'll love this heartfelt novel.

"What a wonderful series! The first book is Cowboy's Reunion. Tricia's story begins in that book. Emotional stories with wonderful characters. Looking forward to the rest of the books in this series." Jutzie - Amazon reviewer

TAMING THE COWBOY

A saddle bronc trying to prove himself worthy to a father who never loved him. A wedding planner whose ex-fiancee was too busy chasing his own dreams to think of hers. Two people, completely wrong for each other who yet need each other in ways they never realized. Can they let go of their own plans to find a way to heal together?

"This is the third book in the series and I have loved them all. . . . can't wait to see what happens with the last sibling." - Amazon reviewer

THE COWBOY'S RETURN

The final book in the Family Ties Series:

He enlisted in the military, leaving his one true love behind.

She gave herself to a lesser man and paid a terrible price.

In their hometown of Rockyview, they can choose to come together or say a final goodbye...

"This author did an amazing job of turning heartache into happiness with realism and inspirational feeling." Marlene - Amazon Reviewer

SWEETHEARTS OF SWEET CREEK

Come back to faith and love

#1 HOMECOMING

Be swept away by this sweet romance of a woman's search for belonging and second chances and the rugged rancher who helps her heal.

#2 - HER HEARTS PROMISE

When the man she once loved reveals a hidden truth about the past, Nadine has to choose between justice and love.

#3 - CLOSE TO HIS HEART

Can love triumph over tragedy?

#4 - DIVIDED HEARTS

To embrace a second chance at love, they'll need to discover the truths of the past and the possibilities of the future...

#5 - A HERO AT HEART

If you like rekindled chemistry, family drama, and small, beautiful towns, then you'll love this story of heart and heroism.

#6 - A MOTHER'S HEART

If you like matchmaking daughters, heartfelt stories of mending broken homes, and fixer-upper romance, then this story of second chances is just right for you.

HOLMES CROSSING SERIES

The Only Best Place is the first book in the Holmes Crossing Series.

#1 THE ONLY BEST PLACE

One mistake jeopardized their relationship. Will surrendering her dreams to save their marriage destroy her?

#2 ALL IN ONE PLACE

She has sass, spunk and a haunting secret.

#3 THIS PLACE

Her secret could destroy their second chance at love

#4 A SILENCE IN THE HEART

Can a little boy, an injured kitten and a concerned vet with his own past pain, break down the walls of Tracy's heart?

#5 ANY MAN OF MINE

Living with three brothers has made Danielle tired of guys and cowboys. She wants a man. But is she making the right choice?

#6 A PLACE IN HER HEART

Her new boss shattered her dreams and now she has to work with him. But his vision for the magazine she loves puts them at odds. Can they find a way to work together or will his past bitterness blind him to future love.